Violence
and the Family

AAAS Selected Symposia Series

Published by Westview Press, Inc.
5500 Central Avenue, Boulder, Colorado

for the

 American Association for the Advancement of Science
1776 Massachusetts Avenue, N.W., Washington, D.C.

Violence and the Family

Edited by Maurice R. Green

AAAS Selected Symposium **47**

AAAS Selected Symposia Series

This book is based on a symposium which was held at the 1979 AAAS
National Annual Meeting in Houston, Texas, January 3-8. The symposium
was sponsored by the American Academy of Psychoanalysis and AAAS
Section J (Psychology).

Published in 1980 in the United States of America by
   Westview Press, Inc.
   5500 Central Avenue
   Boulder, Colorado 80301
   Frederick A. Praeger, Publisher

Library of Congress Cataloging in Publication Data
Main entry under title:
Violence and the family.
   (AAAS selected symposium ; 47)
   "Based on a symposium which was held at the 1979 AAAS national
annual meeting in Houston, Texas, January 3-8."
   Includes bibliographical references and index.
   1. Family violence--United States--Congresses. I. Green, Maurice R.
II. Series: American Association for the Advancement of Science. AAAS
selected symposium ; 47.
HQ809.3.U5V56   362.8'2   80-15809
ISBN 0-89158-841-8

Paperback edition published in 1981 by Westview Press, Inc.
Paperback ISBN: 0-86531-141-2

About the Book

After an introduction to this emotionally charged and
myth-laden topic by a child-and-family psychiatrist, the
authors report and elucidate data on various types of
family violence and suggest that the factors responsible for
most of the violence stem from the use of "morally right"
physical punishment as a method of discipline affirmed over
and over again by social norms and rules. The role of television media in violent behavior is part of a discussion of
the delicate balance of human relationships as a system in
which violence is simply one more unfortunate human propensity. Ethnic and subcultural factors are explored and
new material presented about cultures that do not permit
violence. The last chapter addresses the potential role of
the police in preventing the escalation of violence and in
teaching alternatives to violence-prone families, and includes comments by a police chief who describes the successful application of these techniques.

About the Series

The *AAAS Selected Symposia Series* was begun in 1977 to
provide a means for more permanently recording and more
widely disseminating some of the valuable material which is
discussed at the AAAS Annual National Meetings. The volumes
in this *Series* are based on symposia held at the Meetings
which address topics of current and continuing significance,
both within and among the sciences, and in the areas in which
science and technology impact on public policy. The *Series*
format is designed to provide for rapid dissemination of
information, so the papers are not typeset but are reproduced
directly from the camera-copy submitted by the authors. The
papers are organized and edited by the symposium arrangers
who then become the editors of the various volumes. Most
papers published in this *Series* are original contributions
which have not been previously published, although in some
cases additional papers from other sources have been added
by an editor to provide a more comprehensive view of a
particular topic. Symposia may be reports of new research
or reviews of established work, particularly work of an
interdisciplinary nature, since the AAAS Annual Meetings
typically embrace the full range of the sciences and their
societal implications.

WILLIAM D. CAREY
Executive Officer
American Association for
the Advancement of Science

Contents

About the Editor and Authors

Maurice R. Green, *an assistant clinical professor at Columbia University, also works in the Department of Child and Adolescent Psychiatry at St. Luke's Hospital Center. A specialist in child, family, and forensic psychiatry, he has written several books and numerous articles on identity, communication, the family, and family court. He has served on the National Council on Family Relations, the steering committee of the New York Academy of Family Physicians, and the Committee on the Family of the New York District Branch, American Psychiatric Association.*

Morton Bard *is a professor of psychology at the Graduate Center, City University of New York, and director of the Center for Social Research. His primary interests are crisis intervention, conflict management, and social systems analysis and change, and he originated police training in family crisis intervention. He is the author of* The Crime Victim's Book *(with D. Sangrey; Basic Books, 1979) and* Issues in Law Enforcement: Essays and Case Studies *(with R. Shellow; Reston, 1976), and the script for the award-winning film,* "Death Notification" *(Harper & Row, 1978). He is a fellow of the American Psychological Association and the International Council of Psychologists; in 1975 he received a national award of the American Society for Public Administration.*

Donald A. Bloch, *a practicing psychiatrist for more than 25 years, is currently director of the Ackerman Institute for Family Therapy. During his career he has been director of research for a number of social and psychiatric agencies. He is the author of publications on therapeutic techniques and delinquency and deviant behavior in children, including* Techniques of Family Psychotherapy: A Primer *(Grune & Stratton, 1973). He is a member of the Accreditation Commission for the American Association for Marriage and Family Therapy.*

Lynette K. Friedrich-Cofer *is an associate professor of psychology at the University of Houston, Texas. A specialist on the effects of television on social development, she has published papers on aggression and prosocial television and children's behavior; the use of television in early childhood education and for teaching interpersonal skills to children; and on the perceptions of television heroines by adolescents. She is a fellow of the American Psychological Association and a member of the Board of Editors of* Developmental Psychology.

Curtis E. McClung *has been a member of the Columbus, Georgia, police department since 1950 and has been chief of that department since 1971. He is a former president of the Georgia Association of Chiefs of Police and a member of the Georgia State Crime Commission. He is the recipient of several awards, including the Sertoma International "Service to Mankind" Award (1977) and the "Outstanding Police Chief Award" (1974) from the Georgia Association of Chiefs of Police.*

Dorothy G. Singer *is a professor of psychology at the University of Bridgeport, Connecticut, and codirector of the Yale Family Television Research Center. She has studied both development of language and the effects of television on children and is the author of* Television, Imagination and Aggression: A Study of Preschoolers *(with J. L. Singer; Erlbaum, 1980) and* Teaching Television: Turn Children's Television Programming to Your Child's Advantage *(with J. L. Singer and D. M. Zuckerman; Dial Press, 1981). She is a fellow of the American Psychological Association.*

Jerome L. Singer *is a professor of psychology at Yale University and codirector of the Yale Family Television Research and Consultation Center. He has studied the effects of television on child development; his other research interests include daydreams, imagery, and fantasy. Recently he coauthored* Television, Imagination and Aggression: A Study of Preschoolers *(with D. G. Singer; Erlbaum, 1980) and* Teaching Television: Turn Children's Television Programming to Your Child's Advantage *(with D. G. Singer and D. M. Zuckerman; Dial Press, 1981). He is a former president of the Eastern Psychological Association and is a fellow of the American Psychological Association.*

John P. Spiegel *is a professor of social psychiatry and director of the Training Program in Ethnicity and Mental Health at Brandeis University and is a former director of the Lemberg Center for the Study of Violence. His specialties are social psychiatry, family studies, and ethnicity, and he has published widely on these topics; his books include* Transactions in Families *(with J. Papajohn; Jossey-Bass, 1975) and* Transactions: The Interplay Between the Individual, the Family and Society *(Science House, 1971). A past president of the American Psychiatric Association, he currently serves as president of the Mental Health Film Board, Inc., and on the board of the American Academy of Psychoanalysis.*

Murray A. Straus *is professor of sociology and director of the Family Violence Research Program at the University of New Hampshire. He has published widely on the family, rural sociology, and measurement techniques in sociology. He is the author of* Behind Closed Doors: Violence in the American Family *(Doubleday. 1980) and* The Social Causes of Husband-Wife Violence *(University of Minnesota Press, 1980). He is a former president of the National Council on Family Relations, and in 1977 he received the National Council's Ernest W. Burgess Award for outstanding research on the family.*

Louis Jolyon West *is professor and chairman of the Department of Psychiatry and Biobehavioral Sciences, University of California-Los Angeles, and director of the Neuropsychiatric Institute. He is well known for his systematic integration of the behavioral sciences into medical education. His research has contributed to knowledge in a number of areas, including characteristics and disorders of consciousness, alcoholism, drug abuse, the counter-culture, racism, and violence. He has written or edited six books and has published more than 120 papers, and serves on the editorial boards of several professional journals.*

Foreword

Psychoanalysis and the behavioral sciences in general have been concerned from their beginnings with the problem of violence. Since psychoanalytic theory is based upon the consideration of both conscious and unconscious factors in the dynamics of the family, the symposium findings contained in this volume, illuminating some of the causes and mechanisms of familial violence, make a significant contribution.

As therapists, we are concerned with aggression, whether directed against others or turned back on the self, finding in its violent expression a variety of forces: repressed hostility, pathogenic intrafamily dynamics, biological, social, economic and other factors.

Recent attention to the problems of child abuse and spouse abuse has highlighted the importance of social learning. One finds that children who have been abused by their parents are prone to become abusive parents in their turn. Similarly, spouse abuse often reveals a pattern of identification of victim with aggressor.

Cultural patterns play their part. For example, cultural anthropologists point out that the incidence of murder in one society may be tenfold that of another. Societal and cultural determinants become apparent when we consider the sanctioned, generalized violence of war.

Such considerations make clear the importance of understanding all of the factors that may go to create violent behavior: the individual and psychological determinants, the psychodynamic and psychobiological, the societal and cultural.

This volume, an expression of the joint meetings of the American Academy of Psychoanalysis and the American Association for the Advancement of Science, throws invaluable light on a still dark area of human behavior.

Joe Yamamoto
President, American
Academy of Psychoanalysis

Violence
and the Family

Introduction

Violence in America seems to have been increasing steadily for the past half century, and the same may be said of much of the rest of the western world. The very nature of the violence appears to have changed: it has become more vicious and impersonal. It has risen in all areas of our country and in all social strata. Certainly it has risen in our consciousness, to become a primary issue of social concern. It is a concern that registers heavily, too, on the subliminal register of our personal apprehensions, the security system of the subconscious that bids us bar our windows, cast uneasy glances over our shoulders on deserted platforms, keep to well-lighted streets when out at night.

Unquestionably, violence is much more visible than ever before. It is more vividly and circumstantially reported, more thoroughly studied, more palpable in every walk of life. It looms larger in the collective imagination, and it conditions our lives and social behavior in ways inconceivable to earlier generations.

Our drama, our popular literature, press, podium and pulpit, and the powerfully persuasive mass media of film, radio and television all bring the spectre of epidemic irrational violence home to us. Indeed, here is the crux of the matter. What used to seem remote is now at hand, close, intimate, and threatening.

In the past, the criminal and casual violence of individuals and the violence of sporadic social dissidence both seemed largely confined to sharply delineated social and economic sectors: to the poor, ignorant and alien of slums and shantytowns, to the culturally deprived and politically disinherited, and again to isolated areas of labor strife, racial friction, and radical political agitation. Today the

boiling reservoirs of violence have spilled over their dams.
Violence is in the streets, the marketplace, in the schools
and suburbs, just around any corner.   It pervades all social
strata, exempting no one.   It is at our doorsteps.   It is in
the home.

***

Home is, of course, the locus of the present enquiry.
Violence in the American family is the area of our special
interest.   Since the many questions that relate to violence
in the society at large necessarily also bear on the family,
it seems proper to pursue some of them here, by way of establishing perspective.

For example, it would be helpful to know the extent to
which the current climate of violence reflects a significant,
substantial increase in the incidence of actual violence,
above the level strictly attributable to population growth.
How much, on the other hand, is simply the heightened consciousness of violence that comes of its wider social distribution?   How much is owing to better sampling and more dili-
gant accounting?   How much to the dramatic exploitation, the
sensationalism, of the mass media?   Again, to what extent is
it a matter of changed standards, new sensitivities and new
definitions, reduced tolerance of behavior that, since it
seemed to be class-specific and more or less safely contained, was once accepted as inevitable, like poverty itself?

Common criminal violence is scarcely new in the world.
Footpads and cutthroats were being hanged at Tyburn long before the first "mugger" prowled Central Park.   The gentle-
man's walking stick, like the swordstick and the rapier itself, was a defensive weapon first and a fashion secondarily.
The pocket pistol that was the prerogative of the American
propertyholder throughout the greater part of our history in
most of the country is only now, reluctantly, being surren-
dered.   Armed robbery is not new, nor rape; random violence
is no novelty, nor is familial violence, the battered wife,
the abused child, the murdered infant.

What is new is the social spread of the violence and a
corresponding change in its character, now so often casual,
unpredictable, seemingly irrational in its absence of discernible motive or provocation.

The complex causes of violence change, to be sure, with
the social matrix; with demographic shifts, immigration, ur-
banization, and the conflict of sub-cultures; with altera-

tions in the distribution of wealth and opportunity, and the consequent rise of new aspirations and expectations, creating new frustrations and a new consciousness of social status and deprivation.

Social attitudes have a parallel evolution. New categories of violence, new definitions, come into being with the shift in norms. The legitimate corporal punishment of one era becomes the punishable or censurable abuse of the next, duly reported in the statistics of violence. The kick or the cuff that was the mild reproof of one era or milieu becomes the reportable violence of another. The fisticuffs accepted casually in a given class setting or age group are unacceptable in other circumstances.

Although there is little or no statistical documentation of it, most authorities agree that violence in the family was probably more prevalent and crueler in the past than it is today--almost certainly so as regards the treatment of children. But then, being licit, it did not count as "violence," and rarely became a cause of public concern or social intervention.

Only a generation ago, a black eye was the humorous badge of domestic comedy. Violence between spouses was the staple of the vulgar comic strip. When Jiggs went drinking with his cronies, Maggie was sure to be awaiting his furtive return with folded arms, set jaw, and a rolling pin that said "Pow!" It was considered funny then, and not too great an exaggeration of the folkways of the urban, Irish-immigrant working class. Heightened sensibilities and the diligence of the women's movement cast it in a new light. Increasing social and forensic intervention in the affairs of families, too, provides new insights; the picture changes.

It is by no means a clear picture. For the community of professionals who must interpret it and work with it, from sociologist and caseworker to forensic psychiatrist and judge, it presents a bewildering, complex jigsaw puzzle in which few parts come together and many seem quite incomprehensible, both in their contradictions and for lack of adequate information.

To what extent is intervention itself destructive? To what extent does the conventional family structure--rapidly changing now--contain the seeds of its own destruction? How much of family turmoil is simply a reflection, in microcosm, of the larger social turmoil?

Traditionally the child-rearing function was the responsibility and near-sacred preserve of the parents: clan, community, and church provided monitory support and correction,
ensuring moral and social conformity. Increasingly through
the 19th Century and into the 20th, the schools assumed the
physical, intellectual, and social training and indoctrina-
tion of children--and to some extent of the parents themselves. And increasingly the authority and influence of the
family was weakened as parents became subject to the suasion
of educators, social theorists, the "experts" of the popular
press, and the indoctrinating complex of interests and influences that constitute organized public opinion.

The Oedipal-incest theories of the Freudians, the writ-
ings of the often misguided followers of John Dewey, the developmental charts of Dr. Spock, and Eric Erickson's step-
ladder achievement scale have all had their effect--sometimes
dramatic, often adverse--on the rearing of children, and thus
on the integrity of the family. Feminism and the massive en-
trance of women into the labor force has played its obvious
part. So has the army of behavioral scientists marching under the banners of anti-authoritarianism and family democracy.

The egalitarianism of the age, embedded in the official
rhetoric, has penetrated the family fortress: it fires the
rancorous generational struggle that now reaches downward
from the college campus to the cradle. Children of all ages
today have "rights," asserted by themselves and more convin-
cingly by the attorneys, agencies, and socio-political groups
that speak for them. The family courts listen, legislation
is put forward and adopted, and it develops that children do
indeed have rights, without the quotation marks and often fur-
iously at cross-purposes with the wishes, intentions, and requirements of the adults who are called upon to nurture, edu-
cate, and somehow govern them.

***

All of these factors and a great many more present a formidable field of investigation for the community of professionals who are charged with understanding the violent family
and producing solutions for the problems of its warring members.

As a discipline, the study of intra-family violence is
in its infancy. The surface has scarcely been scratched.
The symposium from which this volume is drawn, conducted
Jan. 3-8, 1979, in Houston, Texas, at the annual meeting of
the American Association for the Advancement of Science in

joint session with the American Academy of Psychoanalysis, represents a decisive step forward in the field.

The symposium data and discussion, presented here verbatim, deal with some of the questions that I have raised directly or tangentially, and throw new light on much besides. The material offers some surprises and some reassurance: for example, the unusually large and sophisticated sampling of 2,143 families on which the Straus report in Chapter 1 is based supports the conclusion that, contrary to the popular impression, there has been no significant increase in the incidence of family violence. As Dr. Straus makes clear, the impression of an "epidemic" of child abuse and wife abuse arises from changing norms of "acceptable" violence and consequent new definitions of what is and is not abuse within these norms. What the apparent epidemic reflects, then, is a new measure of the reportable, arising from the unwillingness of individuals and the community to tolerate a degree of violence that was formerly accepted.

Bloch, innovator, teacher, and practitioner of family therapy, also takes issue with the prevailing tendency to attribute acts of violence within the family to "some pathology" on the part of the aggressor. Most such violence, he seems to find, is "normal" in the sense of arising from the social matrix and being, at root, situational.

Consideration of the social causes of family violence leads naturally to discussion of the role of television—probably the most powerful single socializing agent ever invented—in the conditioning of the young. The subject is treated at length in connection with the work of Jerome and Dorothy Singer; more specifically, in the analysis of data obtained in a year-long Yale group study of the television-viewing habits and linked spontaneous play of preschool children.

Cultural variables in children's attitudes toward violence and in the nature and frequency of violence within families are examined in the symposium contribution of John P. Spiegel, Brandeis professor of social psychiatry. Contrasting the distinct styles of two American sub-cultures, the Italian and the Irish, with the mainstream white Anglo-Saxon Protestant culture, and viewing all three in the light of the traditionally gentle Tahitian way, Spiegel concludes that the suppression of violence, too, has its price. Louis Jolyon West, in the discussion, confronts us with a challenge from the non-violent societies.

When do the police intervene in a family crisis? How do they go about it, and with what effect for good or ill? Police policy and practice is examined by Morton Bard in his study of various successful crisis intervention programs instituted by police departments.

***

A footnote on language: The word <u>aggression</u> is commonly defined as the disposition to employ violent force, or to threaten violence; sometimes it is used to signify the thing itself, and that is the case in some of the symposium papers contained in this volume. The usage flies in the face of the national tendency to applaud certain sorts of aggression, or at any rate aggressiveness: we reward the aggressive salesman, cheer the aggressive fullback, admire the aggressiveness of the Little Leaguer. As a nation, we meet aggression aggressively. No matter. In the context of the symposium, aggression is violence, and all of its variants are equally pejorative, as one might expect of the gentle social scientist. We have, after all, the support of Lorenz himself: he found distinct genetic advantages in violence, but wrote <u>On Aggression.</u>

1. A Sociological Perspective on the Causes of Family Violence

Abstract

This paper gives annual incidence rates for child abuse, spouse abuse, parent abuse, sibling abuse, and for the "normal violence" found in American families. The rates are based on a nationally representative sample of 2,143 families, none of whom are known to be mentally ill. The belief that acts of violence within the family usually reflects some psychopathology on the part of the aggressor is based on the circular reasoning that "anyone who does that must be crazy" and on the "clinical fallacy" in research. Instead, most violence reflects a combination of normal social processes and situations. The major part of the paper describes these social causes. A check list score was computed for each family in the sample based on the presence or absence of 25 indicators of these factors. Violence rates go up exponentially as the check list score increases, as shown by a polynomial correlation of .97. For most people, the violence engendered by these social causes is "normal" or "ordinary" violence such as pushes, slaps, or shoves. This "ordinary" violence and the forms of violence labeled as child-abuse and wife-abuse are two ends of a single continuum. The point on the continuum at which the violence becomes "abuse," and the rates of such abuse, are primarily a reflection of social definitions of what is ordinary or normal, rather than of psychopathology. It has varied widely from one historical period to another. We are now in an historical period in which the "abuse" point on the continuum is being gradually enlarged to include acts of violence which were not previously so defined, thus creating the impression of an "epidemic" of child-abuse and wife-abuse. However, unless a wide range of steps are taken to deal with the basic social causes of violence, the

See Note, page 29.

result of this changing definition may do more to create a
new class of criminals or patients than to reduce the level
of family violence.

Introduction

For the past eight years I have directed a program of
research designed to find out how much physical violence
occurs between members of the same family and why family
members are violent to each other. As a sociologist, I
obviously started with the assumption that much of this
violence grows out of social factors, as contrasted with the
more usual explanations which attribute violence to such
intra-individual factors as aggressiveness, impulsiveness,
or paranoia. (1)

As the work has proceeded, I have been driven to a more
radical sociological perspective. By "a radical sociological
perspective" I mean that I no longer think it is correct to
say that social factors are only one of the sets of factors
which account for intrafamily violence. It is not correct
because putting it this way gives equal weight to non-
social factors such as neurological defects, personality
traits, and psychopathology. Rather than such psychological
factors being anywhere nearly equal in importance to the
social causes of family violence, I am now convinced that
they account for only a miniscule proportion of the violence
which occurs in families--at the outside 10 percent. In
short, at least 90 percent of the violence which takes place
in American families grows out of the very nature of the
family and of the larger society, rather than out of individual aberrations.

Circular Reasoning and Clinical Fallacy

None of what I have just said should be taken to deny
the fact that some men who beat their wives, or some women
who abuse their children are mentally ill. Some are. But
then, so are some truck drivers, some psychiatrists, and
some sociologists. The important point is that to my knowledge there is no evidence that the rate of extreme aggressiveness or the rate of mental illness is any greater among
wife-beaters and child-abusers than it is among truck
drivers, psychiatrists, or sociologists.

If that is the case, what could account for the widespread belief that personality traits and mental illness
account for this violence? There seem to be three reasons:
(1) a simple logical error; (2) what is called the "clinical

fallacy" in research; (3) the individualistic bias of
American culture.

Confounding of Cause and Effect

The logical error is the easiest to deal with. It is
simply the tendency to assume that anyone who "does <u>that</u>"
must be crazy. But this is completely circular reasoning
because the observed effect and the presumed cause are the
same behavior. To demonstrate that mental illness causes
family violence one needs to have independent data on these
traits for a sample that includes both violent and non-
violent persons. With this data one can then determine
if the rate of family violence is any greater among, for
example, the mentally ill, than among the others. To my
knowledge, no such data exist. In fact, the available
evidence suggests that mentally ill people are not more
violent than others (Blumberg, 1974; Gulevich and Bourne,
1970; Kosol, Boucher, and Marofolo, 1972; Melnick and
Hurly, 1969; Mohanan, 1975; and Steadman and Cocozza, 1975).

The Clinical Fallacy

Now let us turn to the "clinical fallacy." Although
there are no data which let us compare the level of family
violence among the mentally ill as compared to others, there
are at least some data which show high rates of psychological
problems among child-abusing parents (Paulson, Afifi, Thompson, and Chaleff, 1974; and Spinetta and Rigler, 1972).
Is this evidence that psychological problems or mental illness cause child abuse? The answer is no. The reason is
that these data refer to people who are being treated for
psychological problems. If they did not have these problems, they would not be under treatment for them. The child
abusers who do not present evidence of mental illness do not
get a chance to be counted in such studies.

Perhaps I can make this more clear with a slightly
different example. Suppose you are a therapist treating
people with sexual dysfunction. Going over your records you
discover that 85 percent of these patients reported that they
grew up in homes in which sex was regarded as "dirty" and in
which talk about sex was forbidden. Does that mean that growing up in a home which represses sex has caused the sexual
dysfunction? Perhaps so, but this is not evidence for such
an assertion. The reason is that any representative cross
section of Americans is likely to show that 85 percent of
them also grew up in homes where sex was regarded as "dirty"
and which prohibited discussion of sex (Rensberger, 1978).

American Individualism

At least one other element is necessary to understand
why there is such a widespread belief that family violence
is due to psychopathology. After all, Americans are certainly not an illogical people, and psychotherapists are
generally familiar with the clinical fallacy. I think the
answer is that there is a culturally based tendency to attribute the cause of behavior to the characteristics of individuals. It is part of the individualistic ethic and values of our society. This is seen most clearly in the case
of socially positive behavior. We assume that if a person
gets ahead in the world and becomes a successful business-
man, successful psychiatrist, or scientist, it is because he
or she is bright, ambitious, and hard-working. We tend to
ignore the fact that most such people come from a family
which values education, can provide financial support for
that education or for getting into business, that they have
grown up in circumstances in which there were rewards for
being ambitious and working hard, got a degree from a high
prestige department, etc.

Similarly, at the negative end of things, if a person
steals, we tend to attribute it to his or her dishonesty.
We forget about such things as whether the person was taught
how to shoplift by other kids, about the vast disparity between the level of affluence which the society trains us to
expect as compared to that which is possible for many, about
the opportunities for theft which might be available as compared to the opportunities to make money by legitimate means,
about the degree to which the person is involved in a socially supportive and socially integrating network of friends
and relatives, and about whether the society treats the person as worthy of respect.

If, somehow, I could strip each of you in this room of
your jobs, of the social supports on which all of you depend
for feelings of self-respect, and at the same time teach you
the basic technical skills for some type of crime, and if you
knew the evidence concerning how much crime is never punished,
it is likely that a large proportion of the "honest" people
in this room would end up committing that crime.

Of course, this is an oversimplified exposition of the
social causes of crime. I simply want to illustrate the fact
that lack of "honesty" is not a cause, but a label applied after the fact to behavior which is largely governed by the life
circumstances in which we find ourselves. In the balance of
this paper, I will attempt to show that this is even more the
case with physical violence by one family member against another.

Violence in a Nationally Representative
Sample of Families

My colleagues and I studied a nationally representative
sample of 2,143 families in order to establish the incidence
rates for such violence in all parts of the country and in
all socioeconomic classes, and in order to estimate the
combined effect of a number of these factors.

Table 1 gives a summary of the main incidence rates.
Those of you who are familiar with rates for violent crimes
such as assaults and homicides know that they are reported
in rates per hundred thousand. By contrast, even without
reading the numbers in this table, you can gain some idea of
just how much violence there is in families from the fact
that the rates in Table 1 are not rates per hundred thousand, nor even rates per thousand. Rather, they are rates
per hundred. Let us look at these figures.

Spouse Abuse

Each year about 16 out of every hundred American couples
experience at least one incident in which either the husband

Table 1. Annual Incidence Rates Per Hundred Couples,
         Parents, or Children, Based on a Nationally
         Representative Sample of American Families
         (N = 2, 143)

Type of Violence	Overall Violence Index*	Severe Violence Index**
Between Spouses	16.0	6.1
Parent-to-Child	63.5	14.2
Child-to-Parent	18.0	9.4
Child-to-Child	79.9	53.2

Source: Straus, Murray A., Richard J. Gelles, and Suzanne
         K. Steinmetz, Behind Closed Doors: Violence in the
         American Family. New York: Doubleday/Anchor, 1979
         (in press).
 * Based on the occurrence of any of the following: throwing
   something at the other person, pushing, grabbing, shoving, slapping, kicking, biting, punching, hitting with
   an object, beating-up, threatening to use a knife or gun,
   using a knife or gun.
** The same list, but excluding throwing things, pushing,
   grabbing, shoving and slapping.

or the wife uses physical force on the other. That is about
one out of every six couples.

As you might expect, most of these violent acts were
minor assaults, such as slapping, pushing, shoving, and throwing things. However, just over six out of every hundred husbands and wives were involved in a more serious act of violence, such as kicking, punching, biting, hitting with an
object, beating up the other, or using a knife or gun. Ap-
plying this rate to the 47 million couples in the United
States suggests that serious violence of this type takes
place in almost three million American homes in a year.
Clearly, the typical American husband or wife stands a much
greater chance of being assaulted in his or her own home
than in walking the streets of even the most crime-ridden
city.

Child Abuse

I will not even bother to give the figures on the ordinary violence which the typical American parent engages
in vis-a-vis his or her children because it is just about universal in infancy and early childhood. Even as late as the
last year in high school, about half of all American parents
hit their children (Straus, 1971).

Turning to acts of violence by parents which are more
serious than slapping, spanking, pushing, shoving, and throwing things, Table 1 shows that 14 out of every hundred children per year are the victims of parental attacks which are
serious enough to fall into our Child Abuse Index. This means
that the parent did one or more of the following: kicked,
bit, punched, hit with an object, beat up the child, or used
a knife or gun. Again, translating this rate into an estimate of actual numbers suggests that each year about six and
a half million children are victims of child abuse.

Some of you may have noticed that "hitting with an
object" was included in the Child Abuse Index. Since many
people consider striking a child with a belt, paddle, or
hair brush as just a more severe type of physical punishment,
and not child abuse, we recomputed the Child Abuse Index
without this. The rates are, of course, lower, but still
astoundingly high--almost four out of every hundred children
per year. Again, translating this rate into estimates of
actual numbers means that each year about 1.7 million children are kicked, bitten, punched, beaten up, or faced a
parent who attacked them with a knife or gun.

Violence By Children

Given this level of violence between the parents, and this level of violence by parents against their children, it should come as no surprise that American children are also extremely violent. Each year, about one out of five (18.0 percent) American children strike a parent. Even if we leave out of the violence index the minor acts of violence--pushing, slapping, shoving, and throwing things--the figures are still high. Almost one out of ten American children attack a parent each year using methods which carry a high risk of causing injury.

Finally, there is the most frequently occurring type of family violence--attacks by one child in a family against a brother or sister. This is so common that some parents worry if it does not happen. "Kids will fight" as they say. And indeed they do. Eight out of ten American children get into a physical fight with a sibling each year. But, this is even more likely to be an underestimate than the other rates because there are certain to have been fights the parent did not know about.

Not only are children more violent to each other than to anyone else, in addition they are the ones most likely to attack in ways that could cause serious injury. Over half of American children do one or more of the following to a sibling each year: kick, bite, punch, hit with objects, beat up a sibling, or attack with a knife or gun.

One final point on incidence rates. As children grow older, their violence rate goes down, but it far from disappears. Taking just the major acts of violence, the rates go from 74 per hundred 3- and 4-year-olds, to 64 per hundred 5- to 9-year-olds, to 47 per hundred 10- to 14-year-olds, and 36 out of every hundred 15- to 17-year-olds.

The Social Causes of Family Violence:
I. Family Organization

These statistics and much other data (Gelles and Straus, 1978; Steinmetz and Straus, 1974) suggest that the family is the most physically violent group or institution that a typical citizen is likely to encounter. Ironically, the family is also the most loving and supportive group or institution. That fact has blinded us from seeing the violent side of family life. How can it be that the family is the locus of both love and violence?

The past eight years of the Family Violence Research Program have revealed a large number of the factors which play a part. Bit by bit we are investigating each of them. In this paper I can identify only some of the most important factors. Then, at the end, I will present some empirical evidence showing that these and other factors are closely associated with the occurrence of violence in the family.

One of the earliest discoveries in the Family Violence Research Program was that the family is the place where most of us learn to be violent. This teaching of violence occurs by several processes, mostly without such an intention, but some intended to train children in violence.

Physical Punishment

Physical punishment is the foundation on which the edifice of family violence rests. I start with this aspect because it is so fundamental. It is the way most people first experience physical violence, and it establishes the emotional context and meaning of violence.

When physical punishment is used, several things can be expected to occur. First, and most obviously, is learning to do or not do whatever the punishment is intended to teach. Less obvious, but equally or more important are three other lessons which are so deeply learned that they become an integral part of one's personality and world view.

The first of these unintended consequences is the association of love with violence. Physical punishment typically begins in infancy with slaps to correct and teach. Mommy and daddy are the first and usually the only ones to hit an infant. For most children this continues throughout childhood and adolescence. The child therefore learns that those who love him or her the most are also those who hit.

Second, since physical punishment is used to train the child or to teach about dangerous things to be avoided, it establishes the moral rightness of hitting other family members.

The third unintended consequence is the lesson that when something is really important, it justifies the use of physical force.

These indirect lessons are not confined to providing a model for later treatment of one's own children. Rather, they become such a fundamental part of the individual's personality and world view that they are generalized to

other social relationships, and especially to the relationship which is closest to that of parent and child: that of
husband and wife.

All of the above suggests that early experience with
physical punishment lays the groundwork for the normative
legitimacy of all types of violence but especially intra-
family violence. It provides a role model for such actions.

None of what I have just said should be taken as indicating that physical punishment causes psychological damage
to the child. On the contrary, the available evidence does
not show a connection between the use of ordinary physical
punishment by parents and psychological problems. It seems
that physical punishment produces people who are perfectly
healthy--mentally or in any other way--but also people who
have learned to use violence as a means of solving problems or expressing anger. This is a major part of the reason
underlying the point made early in this paper: that all but
a miniscule portion of the violence which takes place in
American homes (or for that matter anywhere) consists of
violent acts of people who are as normal psychologically as
you or I.

Observing Violence

We have seen that in American families, almost all children have been the victims of violence, having been a victim
of violence by parents or by siblings. Being a victim
doesn't turn one against violence but teaches it as a value.
It is a powerful pro-violence learning experience for most
people (Carroll, 1977; Owens and Straus, 1975). In addition,
for many children, there is not even the need to generalize
this socially scripted pattern of behavior from the parent-
child nexus in which it was learned to other family relationships. This is because, if our estimates are correct, millions of children can directly observe and role model physical violence between husbands and wives. It is a fairly
thorough training in violence. Also, there is more explicit
training and direct encouragement of violence.

Explicit Training in Violence

Finally, in respect to the way families train people to
be violent, we have to take into account the social context.
Ours is a society with a high rate of violence, both interpersonal violence and organizational violence in the form of
wars and violence by the police. It is inevitable that this
context will be reflected in the family. Parents tend to
deal with children in ways that are roughly consistent with

the type of life they perceive--however dimly--that the child
will live. This link between the organization of society and
the way children are socialized has been demonstrated by Kohn
in respect to class differences in socialization (1969) and
also seemed to explain certain of my own data on physical
punishment (Straus, 1971).

The link between societal violence and family training
in violence is no doubt what lies behind one of the findings
from a survey conducted for the National Commission on the
Causes and Prevention of Violence. Seven out of ten people
in this nationally representative sample of adults agreed
that "It is good for boys to get in a few fist fights when
they are growing up" (Stark and McEvoy, 1970). At the back
of their minds, parents know that their sons will take their
places in a violent world. Of course, the respondents in
the Violence Commission survey were probably not thinking of
fights with other members of the same family. But even if
they were not, such principles spill over from one sphere
of life to another.

The Social Causes of Family Violence: II. Cultural Norms Which Make the Marriage License a Hitting License

I have been describing the typical experiences in the
early lives of most Americans since colonial times. These
experiences and the implicit and explicit principles which
they teach have become crystalized in a set of cultural rules
or norms concerning violence in the family.

When "violence in the family" is mentioned, it evokes
the picture of a child with broken bones or a husband beating up his wife for no good reason. Such instances make up
only a small part of the violence in families. Most family
violence does not enter public consciousness because it is
"normal violence" in the sense that it follows the implicit
rules concerning violence. Any theory purporting to explain human violence must take into account these cultural
rules or norms. These norms specify the conditions under
which violence is and is not appropriate, and the nature of
the violent acts which are legitimate, i.e., tolerated, permitted, or required.

Are there instances of violence within the family which
are "legitimate" or acceptable? There are. In general, the
rule in the family is that if someone is doing wrong and
"won't listen to reason," it is ok to hit. In the case of
children, it is more than just ok. Many American parents
see it as an obligation. Moreover, this principle carries

over to the relationship between husbands and wives (Gelles, 1974; Straus, 1976; Straus and Hotaling, 1979). A hint of that was given above.

In identifying a husband who beats up his wife as violent, I used the phrase "for no good reason." The implication of this phrase is that there can be situations in which there is "a good reason" for a husband to hit his wife and vice versa. In fact, about one out of four Americans explicitly take that view (Stark and McEvoy, 1970). Probably far more agree but do not realize it since this is a taken-for-granted (and therefore unperceived) principle.

What is a "good reason" varies from couple to couple, and from subculture to subculture. But in general, the marriage license is also a hitting license. Of course, like a driving license, there are certain restrictions. One cannot exceed the speed limit with a driver's license, and one cannot inflict "excessive" injury with a marriage license.

Just how much violence is "excessive" in marriage or to discipline children also varies with the individual couple and their subculture. Usually, however, there is a distinction (again, seldom perceived) between "ordinary" spanking, pushing, slapping, and throwing things and "real" violence. At one extreme are some couples for whom even one slap is taken in the same way as if one of us were to slap another member of our department. Such couples are rare. Even more rare--almost non-existent--are parents who never hit their children.

The unperceived norm making violence within the family permissible provided it does not result in wounds which need medical attention emerged clearly in my testimony before the Subcommittee on Science and Technology of the House of Representatives (Straus, 1978c).

MR. SCHEUER. Excuse me. When you talk about violence are you talking about a push or a shove?

DR. STRAUS. I am.

MR. SCHEUER. My concept of family violence has been that somebody slugged someone or something, not just a push or a shove.

DR. STRAUS. Yes. That, I think, is pretty much the widespread view of it. I happen to view any slap, push or shove as violence. If I say

that in the past year, as I did, one out of six
couples have hit each other, and said that's ordinary violence, and you said it's not violence--

MR. SCHEUER. I didn't say that. It seems to me
that most people perceive violence as something
that hurts.

DR. STRAUS. That's true.

MR. SCHEUER. Something that inflicts pain.

DR. STRAUS. Yes. Now if, on the other hand, I
were to say that within the last year, out of all
the committees in the House of Representatives,
that only one out of six committee members hit
other committee members, that would be taken as
evidence of violence, even though no one got
stabbed or beat up. If this were the case, most
people would say those House committees are pretty
violent. But when slaps and shoves occur in the
family there is a tendency, as you were suggesting, for people to discount that, even though they
do not--

MR. SCHEUER. The fact is that House committee
meetings are not violent.

DR. STRAUS. Right.

MR. SCHEUER. And to say that they're violent
is just an abuse of the English language.

DR. STRAUS. I'm sorry I didn't make myself
clear on that. I said, _if_ a rate of violence
such as I had been reporting for ordinary
pushes, slaps and shoves were true of House
committees, one would, as you just said, consider
them very violent.

On the other hand, in the case of families, people
say, "Well, that's just pushing, slapping and
shoving. That's not really violence."

MR. SCHEUER. Well, slapping, a good hard slap,
hurts.

DR. STRAUS. Let's take a mild slap.

MR. SCHEUER. You can break a person's jaw with a slap.

DR. STRAUS. Let's take a mild slap. It doesn't break a jaw; it just stings a little. Is that not violence?

MR. SCHEUER. That's violence.

DR. STRAUS. That's fine. That is my contention also, Mr. Chairman. But that is not the contention of the public in general. I think, that when it refers to families, the public thinks of violence as things that go beyond that: severe kicking, punching, beating up, stabbing, and so forth. So there is an implicit toleration or implicit permission for family members to use milder forms of violence on each other. But for members of university departments or a House committee no one says that "just" pushing or slapping isn't violence.

At the other extreme, are couples for whom physical fights and spanking or slapping a child are a common occurrence. That end of the continuum is also illustrated by the so-called "stitch rule" in many cities. It is an informal understanding among the police that in cases of family fights, no arrest will be made unless there is a wound which requires more than a certain number of stitches. The same principle of tolerating violence except when serious injury is produced or imminent, applies almost universally to parental violence.

Since it is difficult to perceive the fact that there are cultural norms or rules which give permission for family members to hit each other, another example is appropriate: physical fights between children in the family. Only a few parents feel that children should be left to fight things out among themselves. Most parents try to stop such fights and teach children not to hit their brothers and sisters. But in the very process of intervening, each fight between children in a family is typically an implicit but powerful lesson teaching the rule that violence within the family is just part of life, not necessarily a good part, but one that is to be expected.

The reason is that parents react differently than if it was someone else's child who had been punched or kicked by one of their children, or someone else's child who had done that to one of their children. If it is someone else's child, there would be cries of outrage, and possibly even

legal action if the violence persisted. But between their
own children, parents, in effect, tolerate such behavior for
years. It is rationalized by thinking that children lack
control. That is not the case. The data from our research
show that the same children are far more violent to their
own siblings than they are to other children. Moreover,
this continues into the late teen ages. In one of our
samples, 62% of the high school seniors hit a sibling during
the year, but "only" 35% had hit someone outside the family
during that same year.

The Social Causes of Family Violence:
 III. Family Organization

Despite the importance of cultural norms, they are only
part of the story. There are many conflicting and contra-
dictory norms. It also hardly needs to be said that norms
are violated as well as followed. We all do some things we
do not believe in, and fail to do some things we do want to
do. So more than just cultural norms have to be considered.

Obviously, one of the things to consider are individual
differences. Some people are more rule-abiding than others.
Granted the importance of individual differences, our society is so individualistically oriented that we fail to
see that deviation from the norms is also caused by the very
nature of the society itself. In fact, my guess is that the
primary cause of most deviance--including deviant violence--
is to be found in the organization of society.

Social Organization

By social organization I mean the pattern of relationships between individuals and between groups--how the parts
of society are related to each other and to the whole. Some
aspects of social organization are dictated by the culture,
but many are not. For example, bureaucracy is said to have
been highly regarded in imperial Germany, but Americans regard it as an evil. Nevertheless, as a result of the complexity of a high-technology society, bureaucracy is a major
feature of American social organization. Irrespective of
whether one values or denigrates bureaucracy and red tape,
this aspect of social organization has consequences, some
good and some unwanted. The same is true of many aspects
of family organization.

There are many aspects of the way American families are
organized which tend to produce violence, even though that
is no part of their intent. In a forthcoming book (Straus
and Hotaling, 1979) and in a paper on theories of violence

in the family (Gelles and Straus, 1978) many such characteristics are discussed.   There is only space to mention five
of them here.

1. Age and Sex Differences

Let us start with the most fundamental aspect of family
organization. This is the fact that the family consists of
persons of diverse ages and both sexes. What does that have
to do with violence? A lot, because the differences between
what children want and what parents want, and the conflict
between what husbands want and what wives want makes the
family the locus of the "generation gap" and "the battle of
the sexes."

2. Range of Activities and Interests

Conflict in the family is also high because, unlike
special purpose groups (such as academic departments, uni-
versities, or factories), the activities and interests of
a family cover just about everything. Hence there are more
things to get into a hassle about. We even use the term
"paternalistic" to indicate that other groups should not be
involved in every aspect of a person's life in the way a
family is. This means that in addition to the different per-
spectives and interests brought in by men and women, and
by older and younger generations, there are simply more
"events" over which a dispute can develop than is true for
other groups.

3. Intensity of Involvement

Not only is there a wider range of events over which a
dispute or dissatisfaction can occur, and not only does the
mixture of ages and sexes further increase the potential for
such conflicts, but in addition, the degree of injury felt
in such conflicts is likely to be much greater than if the
same issue were to arise in connection with someone outside
the family. Love, paradoxically, gives the power to hurt.

4. Right to Influence

Membership in a family carries with it both a concern
for other members and a right to influence their behavior.
Consequently, the dissatisfaction over undesirable or im-
pinging activities is further heightened by attempts to change
the behavior of the other. If, for example, a colleague
spells or eats incorrectly, that can be mildly annoying, or
more likely, a subject for derision and jokes. But if the
bad spelling or table manners are those of one's child or

spouse, the pain can be excruciating. And if, in addition,
one attempts to correct those table manners, dishes may fly.

5. Family Privacy

The rules of our society make what goes on in the family
a private affair. This aspect of the family system insu-
lates the family from both the social controls and assistance in coping with conflicts. Moreover, even after violence occurs, the rule of family privacy is so strong that
it prevents the victims from seeking help. That is why
Erin Pizzey's book on wife-beating is called <u>Scream Quietly
or the Neighbors Will Hear</u> (1974).

What are the implications of these five aspects of
family organization? Few would say that the family should
not consist of people of mixed ages and sexes, that it
should not encompass the whole of life, that family members
should not be intensely involved and committed to the family,
that family members should not have a right to influence
other family members, or that there should be no family privacy. Ironically, these are all desirable aspects of family
organization; <u>and they are also aspects which generate a
high level of conflict</u>.

Stress, Power, and Violence
in the Family

There are ways of coping with, even if not changing,
the aspects of family organization I have just identified
(Straus, 1977; 1978a). There are also aspects of family
organization which contribute to violence, on which there
is a wide agreement about the need for change. Among these
are the high level of stress experienced as part of membership
in a family, and <u>the balance of power between husband and
wife</u>.

High Level of Stress

Family relationships tend to generate many stresses.
This comes about because of a number of circumstances, starting with the general tendency for all dyadic relationships
to be unstable (Simmel, 1955:118-144). In addition, the nuclear family continuously undergoes major changes in structure as a result of processes built into the family life
cycle: events such as the birth of children, aging, and
retirement. The crisis-like nature of these changes has long
been recognized (LeMasters, 1957).

Finally, there are the stresses inherent in what is expected of families. For example, families are expected to provide adequate food, clothing and shelter in a society which does not always give families the resources necessary to do this. Also stressful is expectation that families bring up healthy, well-adjusted, law-abiding, and intelligent children who can get ahead in the world. The stress occurs because these traits, and the opportunity to get ahead, are all factors which are to a greater or lesser extent beyond the control of any given family.

In a recent paper I tested the theory that the level of family violence is a function of the amount of stress experienced by the family (Straus, 1978b). The results provided clear evidence that the more stress the family was under, the higher the probability of violence between husband and wife.

Sexual Inequality

Despite the change to a more equalitarian system, the balance of power in American marriages still rests with the husband. This fact is obscured by an equalitarian rhetoric, so one has to look at the objective evidence to see the actual balance of power. For example, if the husband can get a promotion by moving to a different city, the chances are much greater that the family will move than if a move is needed for the wife to get a better job.

The husband as the "head of the family" remains the presumption of our legal system, despite some recent changes. This is also the presumption in countless administrative rulings and procedures. For example, the first two questions in the 1970 census asked for the "Name of the head of the household" and then for the "Wife of head."

There are many social rules which give men advantages which enable them to be dominant in the family. Women employed full time earn only 57 percent of the salaries of full-time employed men. But it starts well before that in the principle that a man should marry a woman who is younger than he is, less well educated, and shorter. All of these are resources for exercising power, as recognized in such folk sayings as "Money talks," "Older and wiser," "Knowledge is power," etc.

What about the last of the advantages I mentioned: the expectation that a man should marry a woman who is shorter. The fact that women average about three inches less height than men is a biological reality. But the rule that

men should be taller than their wives is a cultural norm,
which, in my opinion, reflects the "need" for men to have
the ultimate resource of physical force to back up their
authority. As a husband in one of the families interviewed
by LaRossa (1977) said when asked why he hit his wife during
an argument:

> She more or less tried to run me and I said no,
> and she got hysterical and said, "I could kill
> you!" And I got rather angry and slapped her in
> the face three or four times and I said "Don't
> you ever say that to me again!" And we haven't
> had any problem since.

The point is that a great deal of family violence occurs because men grow up thinking they have the right to
the final say in family matters. Yet despite the advantages
which society gives to men, many men lack the greater economic resources and superior personal qualities needed to
justify such privilege. As the husband I just quoted illustrates, and as shown in a statistical data of 385 families
(Allen and Straus, 1979), this is truly an explosive combination. Such men are very likely to use physical violence
to show her "who's who around here."

The Interaction of Culture, Social Organization, and Social Learning

But it is not just the high level of conflict inherent
in the organization of families which produces violence.
There is also a high level of conflict in academic departments. Yet instances of physical violence are extremely
rare in academic life. The worst that I can remember in
30 years and five different departments is a department
meeting at which someone threw an eraser at the wall. Obviously, something in addition to a high level of conflict is
needed to explain the frequency of physical violence in
families.

The explanation lies in the combined effect of the three
factors discussed in this paper: (1) the high level of
conflict in families; (2) the training in violence and
the link between love and violence established by physical
punishment; and (3) the implicit cultural norm which gives
family members the right to hit if someone is "doing wrong"
and "won't listen to reason."

That combination sets the stage for the fact that at
some time or other, violence occurs in most families. This
is because there are times when we are all wrongdoers and

"do not listen to reason." Thus, even though some family
violence can be traced to neurological and psychological
disturbances, such factors are a miniscule part of the picture. Rather, almost all the violence which is endemic in
American families is a product of the very nature of the
society and the family itself.

Putting the Pieces Together

In this paper I have tried to show that most violence
in families reflects a combination of normal process and
situations. Among these are: (1) The learned association
between love and violence which is established from infancy
on through the use of physical punishment. (2) The moral
rightness of family members using physical force when another
person does wrong and persists in it: the "I deserved it"
pattern. (3) The belief (especially strong in the family,
but also present in the society at large) that if a person
persists in wrongdoing and other things fail, physical
force is both legitimate and expected. (4) The crystaliza-
tion of the previous three factors into a taken-for-granted,
and therefore largely unperceived, norm which gives family
members the right to hit each other. (5) The socially
structured antagonism between the sexes and between generations. (6) The assignment of family responsibilities and
obligations on the basis of age and sex rather than on the
basis of competence and interest, and especially one specific
aspect of this: (7) The expectation that the husband will
be the "head of the household" and therefore the "need" to
maintain that by force if necessary. (8) The lack of alternatives and ability to escape from a violent family. This
is most apparent in the case of children, but it also applies
to wives, and to a lesser extent to husbands. (9) The high
level of violence in other spheres of life which carries
over into the family, for the most part unconsciously,
but sometimes explicitly, as in the belief of most parents
that it is good for boys to get into occasional fist fights.
(10) The frustration which (along with opportunities) are
built into our economic system, especially for the millions
of families living below the poverty line, and the unemployed.
(11) The social isolation of millions of families from a
network of kin and community which can help resolve family
problems and conflicts and also act as agents of social
control.

Up to this point, each of the causal factors just listed
was considered separately from the others. Also, the empirical evidence for each of the factors was presented infor-
mally, or by citing previous papers. This may be plausible
to some, but it is not a substitute for concrete evidence.

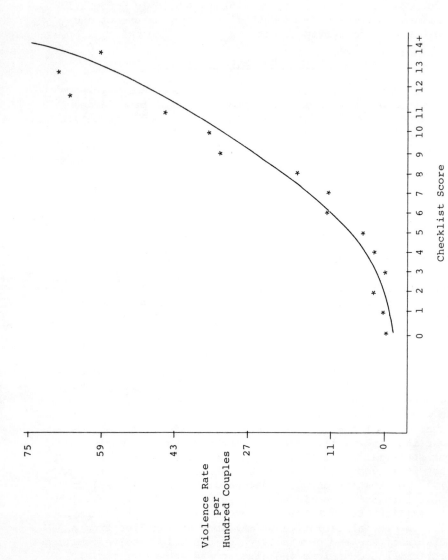

Figure 1.   Couple Violence Rate by Checklist Score

Especially needed is evidence which takes into account the combined effect of these factors.

To really get at the combined effect of the social factors described in this paper we need to nail down cause and effect relations by tracing families over time. We would also need to use statistical methods which take into account the effect of different combinations of causal factors. That is the kind of study we are now planning. In the meantime, however, I can give the results using just the cross-sectional data, and simply adding together the presumed causal factors. Even that is impressive.

These data are from a forthcoming book, Behind Closed Doors: Violence in the American Family (Straus, Gelles and Steinmetz, 1979). The procedure was to give each of the 2,143 families in the national survey a "Checklist" score. A family got one point for each characteristic associated with a higher than average rate of husband-wife violence. For example, if the husband experienced more than the average amount of physical punishment when growing up, one point was assigned. If the balance of power in the family was lop-sidedly male-dominant, another point was added. If the couple experienced a high number of stressful events, such as unemployment, we added another point to their score. Altogether, a couple's score could range from zero (for those who had none of these characteristics) to 25, for those who had all of them. Fortunately, none of the couples lived under the burden of all 25. The scores ranged from zero (seven couples), to 18 (two couples), with an average of six characteristics per couple.

If the theory that the combined effect of the social factors included in this Checklist does account for the fact that some families are violent and others are not, those with zero or near zero scores should have a violence rate of zero, whereas all or almost all of those with many of these social characteristics should be violent. That is almost exactly what Figure 1 shows.

The asterisks plotted in Figure 1 are the actual violence rates for each Checklist score group. You can see that these rates start with zero for the couples who had none or only one of these characteristics and go up to rates of 64, 68, and 58 per hundred couples with highest scores on the Check-list.

The plotted line is the second degree polynomial regression. The actual violence rates fit this curve very closely, and this is confirmed by the polynomial correla-

tion of .975. The Checklist characteristics therefore
account for 95 percent of the variance in rates of husband-
wife violence. However, it is important to keep in mind
that this is not the same thing as 95 percent of the individual to individual variation in violence. Aggregated data,
such as that in Figure 1, disregards the individual differences at each of the points plotted. What we have explained
is 95 percent of the variation in <u>rates</u>, not of individual
behavior.

Normal Violence, Child Abuse, and Spouse Abuse

In <u>Behind Closed Doors</u> there are other graphs showing
similar relationships with child abuse and severe violence
between spouses. The essential similarity in factors which
account for the ordinary violence of family life and the
violence which is severe enough to be considered child abuse
or wife beating is one of the reasons for thinking of physical punishment and child abuse as simply less and more extreme forms of the same behavior, rather than as evidence
of normal behavior versus psychopathology. In fact, whether
an individual case comes to public attention and is recorded
as an instance of child abuse is often a matter of chance.
It depends on whether a child who has been thrown against
the wall bounces off (as happens most of the time) or whether
a concussion or other serious damage resulted.

More generally, the point on the continuum of violence
at which an act of family violence is regarded as "abuse"
(and the publicly recorded instances and rates of such abuse),
for the most part reflects contemporary social definitions
of what is acceptable. The proper response to statistics
showing huge year to year growth in rates of child abuse
should be to rejoice. Such statistics do not indicate
that there is any more child abuse now than there was five,
ten, or one-hundred years ago. If anything, there is probably less.

What the ever-increasing statistics on child abuse
indicate is a changing standard of family relationships.
We are no longer willing to tolerate the level of violence
to which children have been subjected for centuries. We
are starting to set up systems for identifying and helping
families which exceed the currently permissible level of
violence. The same thing is beginning to happen in respect
to spouse abuse, largely as a result of the women's movement.

In conclusion, I suggest that American society is now
in an historical period in which the "abuse" part of the

continuum is being gradually enlarged to include acts of violence which were not previously so defined. This creates the misleading impression of an "epidemic" of child abuse and wife abuse. However, unless a wide range of steps are taken to deal with the basic social causes of violence, the result of this changing definition may do more to create a new class of criminals or a new class of patients than to reduce the level of family violence.

Notes and References

This paper is one of a series of publications of the Family Violence Research Program at the University of New Hampshire. The program is supported by the University of New Hampshire and by NIMH grants MH27557 and T32 MH15161. A program bibliography and list of available publications will be sent on request.

1. For the purpose of this paper, violence is defined as "an act carried out with the intention of, or perceived as having the intention of, physically hurting another person" (Gelles and Straus, 1978). The "physical hurt" can range from slight pain, as in a slap, to murder. Although this is the basic definition of violence, it is usually also necessary to take into account a number of other characteristics of these violent acts, such as whether it is "instrumental" to some other purpose or "expressive," i.e., an end in itself; and whether it is a culturally permitted or required act versus one which runs counter to cultural norms (legitimate versus illegitimate violence). Thus, the basis for the "intent to hurt" may range from concern for a child's safety (as when a child is spanked for going into the street) to hostility so intense that the death of the other is desired. The former would be an example of "legitimate instrumental violence" and the latter of "illegitimate expressive violence."

Allen, Craig, and Murray A. Straus. Resources, power, and husband-wife violence. Chapter 12 in Straus and Hotaling, 1979.

Blumberg, M. L. Psychopathology of the abusing parent. American Journal of Psychotherapy, 1974, 28, 21-29.

Carroll, Joseph C. The intergenerational transmission of family violence: the long-term effects of aggressive behavior. Aggressive Behavior, 1977, (3), 289-299.

Gelles, Richard J. Child abuse as psychopathology: a sociological critique and reformulation. American Journal of Orthopsychiatry, 1973, 43 (July), 611-621. Also reprinted in Steinmetz and Straus, 1974.

Gelles, Richard J. The Violent Home: A Study of Physical Aggression Between Husbands and Wives. Beverly Hills: Sage, 1974.

Gelles, Richard J. The social construction of child abuse. American Journal of Orthopsychiatry, 1975, 44 (April), 363-371.

Gelles, Richard J., and Murray A. Straus. Determinants of violence in the family: Toward a theoretical integration. In W. Burr, R. Hill, F. I. Nye, and I. Reiss (Eds.), Contemporary Theories About the Family. New York: Free Press, 1978.

Gulevich, G. D., and P. G. Bourne. Mental illness and violence. In D. N. Daniels, M. F. Gilula, and F. M. Ochberg (Eds.), Violence and the Struggle for Existence. Boston: Little, Brown and Co., 1970.

Kohn, Melvin L. Class and Conformity: A Study of Values. Homewood, Ill.: Dorsey Press, 1969.

Kosol, H., R. Boucher, and R. Marofolo. The diagnosis and treatment of dangerousness. Crime and Delinquency, 1972, 18, 371-392.

LaRossa, Ralph E. Conflict and Power in Marriage: Expecting the First Child. Beverly Hills, Calif.: Sage, 1977, Chapter 4.

LeMasters, Ersel E. Parenthood as crisis. Marriage and Family Living, 1957, 19 (November), 352-355.

Melnick, Barry and John R. Hurly. Distinctive personality attributes of child-abusing mothers. Journal of Consulting and Clinical Psychology, 1969, 33 (6), 746-749.

Mohanan, John. The prediction of violence. In Duncan Chappell and John Mohanan (Eds.), Violence and Criminal Justice. Lexington, Mass.: Lexington Books, 1975.

Owens, David M., and Murray A. Straus. The social structure of violence in childhood and approval of violence as an adult. Aggressive Behavior, 1975, 1, 193-211.

Paulson, Morris J., A. Afifi Abdelmonen, Mary L. Thompson, and Anna Chaleff. The MMPI: A descriptive measure of psychopathology in abusive parents. Journal of Clinical Psychology, 1974, 30 (July), 389-390.

Pizzey, Erin. Scream Quietly or the Neighbors Will Hear. Baltimore, Maryland: Penguin Books, 1974.

Rensberger, Boyce. Behavioral study indicates many parents don't tell children of erotic aspects of sex. The New York Times, December 17, 1978, pg. 30.

Simmel, Georg. Conflict and the Web of Group Affiliations. Glencoe, Ill.: Free Press, 1955 (1908).

Spinetta, John J., and David Rigler. The child-abusing parent: a psychological review. Psychological Bulletin, 1972, 77, 296-304.

Stark, Rodney, and James McEvoy III. Middle class violence.
    Psychology Today, 1970, 4 (November), 52-65.
Steadman, Henry J., and Joseph J. Cocozza. Stimulus/response:
    we can't predict who is dangerous. Psychology Today,
    1975, 8, (January 8), 32-35.
Steinmetz, Suzanne K. and Murray A. Straus. Violence in the
    Family, New York: Harper and Row (originally published
    by Dodd, Mead and Co.), 1974.
Straus, Murray A. Some social antecedents of physical pun-
    ishment: a linkage theory interpretation. Journal
    of Marriage and the Family, 1971, 33 (November),
    658-663. Also reprinted in Steinmetz and Straus, 1974.
Straus, Murray A. Sexual inequality, cultural norms, and
    wife-beating. Victimology, 1976, 1 (Spring), 54-76.
    Also reprinted in Emilio C. Viano (Ed.), Victims and
    society. Washington, DC: Visage Press, 1976; and in
    Jane Roberts Chapman and Margaret Gates (Eds.), Women
    into wives: The legal and economic impact of marriage.
    Sage Yearbooks in Women Policy Studies, Vol. 2.
    Beverly Hills, Cal.: Sage, 1977.
Straus, Murray A. A sociological perspective on the preven-
    tion and treatment of wife-beating. In Maria Roy (Ed.),
    Battered Women, New York: Van Nostrand-Reinhold, 1977.
Straus, Murray A. The social causes of interpersonal vio-
    lence: the example of family violence and Odyssey
    House non-violence. Paper presented at the 1978 meet-
    ing of the American Psychological Association,
    Toronto, 1978a.
Straus, Murray A. Stress and assault in a national sample
    of American families. Paper presented at the Col-
    loquium on Stress and Crime, National Institute of
    Law Enforcement and Criminal Justice--MITRE Corporation.
    Washington, D.C. (December 5), 1978b.
Straus, Murray A. National survey of domestic violence:
    some preliminary findings and implications for future
    research. Paper presented at hearing on "Research Into
    Domestic Violence," U.S. House of Representatives,
    Committee on Science and Technology (February), 1978c.
Straus, Murray A., Richard J. Gelles and Suzanne K. Stein-
    metz. Behind Closed Doors: Violence in the American
    Family. Garden City, N.Y.: Doubleday/Anchor, 1979.
Straus, Murray A. and Gerald T. Hotaling (Eds.). The Social
    Causes of Husband-Wife Violence. Minneapolis:
    University of Minnesota Press, 1979 (In press).

Donald A. Bloch

Discussion:
Violence in the Family

I would like to begin my remarks by pointing to an area of disagreement that I have with the model that Dr. Straus has used. I think it is a linear causality model, where one tries to find causes at each level of analysis that allow the distribution as he made it, let us say, between 90% sociological causes and 10% intrapsychic causes. Since my work is directly with families and is at a middle level of abstraction and generality--that is, somewhere between the intrapsychic and interpersonal and the larger sociological level of analyses--I find that that kind of distribution already sets up a sort of orientation in which there get to be fights over intellectual territories and domains. From my perspective, that is unnecessary. The issue of etiology is not to be decided by a distribution between, let us say, sociologic and intrapsychic causes, but really by an agreement that this is a line of argument that leads nowhere: that any human event has manifestation at all levels, even neurological organization levels, molecular biological levels, organ levels, certainly psychological small group and larger group levels. Therefore, in dealing with a topic of this sort, it seems we are better advised not to get into that kind of concern, but rather to address ourselves to an understanding of the representation of violence or other sorts of issues of that sort at all of these levels, without trying to look for causal or primary causal or major causal kinds of explanations.

I do think there is an enormously important polemical point that lies behind the approach that Dr. Straus takes-- i.e., that he wants to say to us that violence is not to be segregated or scapegoated or defined as some kind of special problem--either psychopathological or criminal, for that matter--but rather--I think we would agree--that it represents a human propensity that represents a feature of

the response set of the ways of reacting to disequilibria
that occur in all humans.

In reading the paper and thinking about it, I have tried
to imagine myself as a respondent to this survey. None of
us are exempt from violence and that, then, leads me to
my personal recollections that perhaps will illustrate what
I am talking about. The other day I almost committed child
abuse. The circumstances were these: I was playing with
my two-year-old, who is a happy, cheerful, and engaging
little fellow. As we were romping, I realized that, in a
fraction of a second, the following sequence had taken place:
In his exuberance he had bitten me very hard on my stomach.
And, before I knew what had happened, I had grabbed him,
held him up, and almost done something abusive.

That made me recollect another event with a couple of
other kids: a seven-year-old child was watching television
when the other, a five-year-old, crossed in front of his
path, whereupon again--these events took place in about
two or three milliseconds--the five-year-old crossing in
front of his brother was tripped and went splat. I'm quite
sure that before he hit the deck I had his brother by
the back of the neck and had spanked him. Now I assure you
that this class of event is rare in our house. It just
is not what goes on. Nevertheless, I think it is instructive. It is instructive because I had to be aware of
this immediate, intense and violent reaction, in both instances quite rapidly, and function in what I would think
of as a disequilibrium model--i.e., a model that also has to
do with maintenance of boundaries. In one instance, the
boundary was my stomach, which was invaded by this happy
little bite. The other was a set of boundaries that had to
do with the seven-year-old television watcher. When I
grabbed and spanked him, he went upstairs and cried for
a bit; a little later I went up to comfort him. What he
said to me was, "Daddy, I just don't know what happened.
I tripped Jeremy before I even knew what I was doing."
And I said, "Yes, and I had you by the back of the neck
spanking you before I knew what I was doing." Now if we
had been surveyed in that year, we would have had child
abuse or hitting. We would have had sibling-to-sibling violence and quite properly so.

I am emphasizing this point because I think that there
is a moral issue here, in addition to all of the other kinds
of issues, conceptual, clinical and otherwise. The moral
issue is that we are all owners of this response set. The
clinician cannot work with a violent family if the clinician

sets herself or himself in some way apart. If the clinician
approaches a child-abusing mother without a sense that she/
he is a potential child-abuser, or in fact is, then the conditions of the work—and I think also the conditions of the
investigation—are badly damaged. In that sense, then,
I would strongly support what I take to be the polemical
and political point that lies behind the approach that Dr.
Straus has put before us. At the same time, though, I feel
that I would like to urge against getting caught in questions
of whether something is normal or not normal, psychopathological or not: those are mostly territorial wars that we
could probably get along without.

There are questions, then, about what are the <u>character-
istics of families that lie at the extreme end of the continuum of violence proneness</u>. Undoubtedly, such a continuum
exists. The nature of those characteristics determines both
the social moves, the kinds of social interventions, as well
as the kinds of clinical moves that one may make. <u>Strategies</u>
for reducing violence-proneness have to grow out of our understanding of the nature of these families and their special characteristics. I am suggesting—and I do not think
that this is a contradiction of Dr. Straus's point—that
it is very necessary for us to have a <u>typology of violent
families</u> and to understand something about those characteristics of people at the extreme end of the continuum. And,
in a few minutes here, I would like to suggest a few. Let
me emphasize again that this does not in any way contradict
his findings. In fact, I think I can tie what I am going
to say to the <u>sociological level of analysis</u>. I may not have
enough time here to fully do that, but I want to make clear
that this is my perspective.

For example, as clinicians, we find violent families to
be authoritarian and sexist. You can describe the <u>role
structure</u> in many such families as being brittle and rigid;
they have a very limited interpersonal repertoire. The
number of moves that they can make—if you simply quantify
them or if you take the range of <u>interpersonal operations</u>
within the family (and these, of course, are critical in
regard to interpersonal operations involved in child-rearing)—you are dealing with people at the extreme end, with
people who have a restricted internal role repertoire and a
restricted series of interpersonal moves within the family.
They quite literally do not know anything else to do as
a response to stress, and the statement, "The kid's going
to do this; what else is there to do except hit him?", is
really about a kind of impoverishment of familial social
options. The notion does not occur that one could, let us

say, talk gently to a child, that one could put some increase
in negative stimulus in one's voice, as opposed to hitting.
These patterns go down through the generations: nobody has
learned how to do more things.

In addition, these families have a limited external
social repertoire. Their whole perception of the world,
their whole ability to organize their own place in the
world, to have the ability, for example, to use the range
of economic and social support systems that are available--
their limitations are great. These are characteristics both
of something that goes on within the family and something
that goes on external to the family, and they might help
us develop a typology associated with this. These are
families with low self-esteem; they are families that feel
shamed, worthless and, indeed, occupy lower places in any
social scale. Although violence occurs at all class levels,
as one moves down the scale of occupational, economic or
other kinds of indices, the rate of violence goes up. These
are under-cared-for families. They are families that are
impoverished economically, educationally, in their psychological resources, and in terms of their ability to function in
the world. They could be characterized as coerced families.
They are families most of whose lives are led in response
to reasons they know not why. They have little ability to
conceptualize the universe or their place in it. They are
frequently enormously uninformed, having never even traveled
beyond their immediate neighborhoods or the immediate social
group of which they are a part. They have no sense about
history and no sense about the range of things that have led
to this particular moment in time, so that most of what they
are doing--and again, it is an extreme generalization, but
I want to put the thoughts before you--most of what they are
doing is a response to being powerless and coerced on the
job, being powerless and coerced in terms of the institutions with which they deal. As a potent example, they deal
with the educational institutions that care for their
children in a shamed way. Thus, the institutions perform
violence upon them. It may not be physical violence, but
there is certainly social and psychological violence.

Also, we could call them under-parented families. And
this takes us into the issue of generational themes. These
are families where, characteristically, the pattern of
poor parenting, of sparse, deficient, fragmented, isolated--
frequently institutional--parenting is very characteristic
of the lives of the parents themselves and, if you look back
and see this generational progression through time, you
realize that you are dealing with something that, among

other things, has a multi-generational character that moves
through time with a set of learned patterns that then provide
no way out, because the violence--in this sense--is the only
available response to ways in which the small family system
is stressed or disequilibrated. I think that I will stop
at this point. There is always a great deal more to say
and I hope that we will have a chance to discuss it, because
it is a very fascinating and interesting theme and I think
we have gotten a good start from Dr. Straus.

Jerome L. Singer, Dorothy G. Singer

2. Television Viewing, Family Style and Aggressive Behavior in Preschool Children

Abstract

This paper summarizes results of television-viewing patterns and spontaneous play behavior of 141 preschool children
followed over a year's time. Results of family interviews
with parents of children showing extremes of TV watching and
aggressive behavior are included.

Theoretical Background and Previous Research

The best available evidence on the development of aggression in children derives from studies that indicate that
family patterns are critical in the emergence of violence.
Children who have been exposed to at least one and often two
parents who themselves are physically aggressive or who have
participated as witnesses or victims in situations involving
rejection or brutalization in the home turn out themselves
to be more likely to be aggressive or antisocial. The absence of opportunities for learning alternative forms of
coping with frustration other than through the socially
supported means of aggression combined with indices of parental aggression or rejection prove to be the most effective
predictors that children will become aggressive in later life
(McCord, McCord, & Howard, 1970; Lefkowitz, Eron, Walder &
Huesmann, 1977). Broader sociocultural evidence for particular patterns of violence such as those that can clearly be
demonstrated in regions of the United States in which the
ratio of homicides to suicides is much higher than elsewhere (Graham & Gurr, 1969) further support the implications
of the social learning or cognitive analysis of the nature of
aggression.

This research was supported by a grant from the National
Science Foundation, APR Program, #6-20772.

Without minimizing for a moment the important factors of parental example or cultural support for overt violence and aggression in children, it can also be maintained that exposure of children and adolescents to extensive demonstrations of violence on the television set in the home may add further to the likelihood that particular children will show an increment in aggressive behavior. In a sense, it can be argued for the child for the past two decades that television may be considered "a member of the family." (J. Singer & D. Singer, 1975). The young American child not only grows up with the behavioral modeling examples of parents as well as language and expressive content presented by the family figures, he or she also lives in an environment in which the television set presents a constant source of stimulation.

Bandura (1973) has carried out the most careful and detailed theoretical analysis of the nature of aggression from the standpoint of social learning theory. His extensive experimental work **has indicated very clearly** that children do imitate observed acts of aggression whether carried out by live adults or filmed models. One can also argue that television not only demonstrates various forms of attacking other people, but that it may reduce some of the sensitivities to pain in others which most of us share to some degree (Cline, Croft, & Courrier, 1973). It may also provide a basic moral support for violence since in program after program the "good guy" usually ends up physically assaulting or shooting the "bad guy" (J. Singer & D. Singer, 1975). The work of Tannenbaum and Zillmann(1975) and of Watt & Krull (1977) also suggests that the high rate of activity and arousal value of the TV may also predispose heavy viewers of the medium, especially children, to aggressive action.

The evidence reviewed by Bandura (1971; 1973) and by Baron (1977) makes it clear enough that at a theoretical level the type of aggressive content presented on television can indeed be imitated by children. Other studies involving relatively brief periods of exposure under controlled conditions also indicate that children will increase the level of aggression following daily viewings of a film like Batman (Friedrich & Stein, 1973). Studies by Noble, (1970, 1973, 1975) also point to such outcome in short-term controlled studies of children's play following exposure to aggressive film. The research evidence accumulated in the studies supported by the Surgeon-General's Committee on Television and Social Behavior (Murray, Rubinstein, & Comstock, 1972) also supported the general view that children predisposed to be aggressive may increase the level of violence after exposure to aggressive material on television.

Field studies carried out by Bailyn (1959), Chaffee (1972), and Schramm, Lyle, & Parker (1961) have all followed up children over longer periods of time and related their television viewing to measures of overt aggressive behavior. In general, these studies do show positive correlations on the order of .25 between TV viewing and the occurrence of aggressive behavior. While clearly these correlations are modest, they do point out that of all of the many possible causes of aggression in children, there is at least some evidence that television contributes to some degree if by no means in a major fashion.

The most telling study to date has been that reported by Lefkowitz, Eron, Walder & Huesmann (1977). This research involved a ten year follow-up of boys and girls originally studied in the third grade. They found that for boys those who were more aggressive turned out to be more regular viewers of aggressive material on television. They also found that "the greater was the boy's preference for violent television at age nine, the greater was his aggressiveness both at that time and ten years later. The boy's preference for violent television correlated .21 (p<.01) with its concurrent peer-rated aggressiveness and .31 (p<.001) with his aggressiveness ten years later" (Lefkowitz et al., 1977, pp. 115-116). In effect, these authors have predicted that one of the best single predictors at the age of nine of whether a boy will later turn out to be rated as aggressive by peers or by other criteria ten years later is the amount of violent television programming he is watching in childhood. It is important to note that these researchers went to great lengths to rule out possible mediating effects of intelligence, social class or family background as a means of explaining the correlation between violent TV viewing and subsequent aggression.

More recently, Belson (1978) has studied a group of boys in England between the ages of 12 and 17 and has followed their TV viewing patterns and aggressive behavior over a period of time. Belson's evidence also suggests that the watching of aggressive material on television, particularly that associated with relatively realistic violent activity rather than slapstick comedy or cartoons, is associated with aggressive behavior.

A Study of Preschoolers' TV Viewing and Aggressive Behavior

A study to be described here is a formed part of a larger examination of the relationship between television viewing patterns and spontaneous play in nursery schools of three- and four-year-old children followed over a year's time. The intention of looking at three- and four-year-olds was to obtain a group of relative "novices" to both the TV viewing experience and the situation of regular social inter-action provided by beginning nursery school and daycare center attendance. In a sense, with respect to the relationship of television and aggression, one might view our approach as something like that of a detective looking for the conclu-sive evidence, the "smoking gun" which might ultimately im-plicate TV as a causal influence in aggression.

Participants

The broader study involved 141 children with approxi-mately equal numbers of boys and girls and of both sexes who were attending daycare centers and nursery schools in the New Haven area. Children were predominantly white, although there was sufficient variability of social class and ethnic background in the sample to yield significant correlational data when those social background factors were included in data analyses. The sample was predominantly lower to middle class in socioeconomic status.

General Procedure

The longitudinal study over a year's time involved two major sources of data. One of these was the maintenance by parents of logs of the television viewing patterns of their children. These logs were kept daily for two week periods four different times during the year. Thus, there were two weeks of log keeping in February 1977, April 1977, October 1977, and February 1978.

During the same "probe periods" in which parents were keeping home logs of children's TV viewing, the children themselves were being observed during spontaneous play in the nursery school or daycare settings. Observations were carried out by pairs of observers who were blind to the ex-perimental hypothesis or to the general backgrounds of the children. There were two observations within a given probe period for each child, making a total of eight independent observations of the child over a year's time.

The child was observed for ten minutes. The observers recorded independently in detail the actual behavior of the child and his or her verbalization. Immediately following a series of observations, the observers then proceeded to rate the child on a number of dimensions, such as imaginativeness of play, positive affect, aggression, etc. These ratings were on a 1-5 scale and were based on definitions provided by the experimenters. Consensus of use of the definition had been obtained through a series of earlier training sessions with the observers. Reliabilities of observer pairs were tested during training and during actual observations and proved to be highly statistically significant.

Children were also interviewed and given some brief tests of intelligence and of predisposition to imagination, e.g., the Rorschach Inkblot in modified form, (Barron Movement blots), questions about imaginary playmates, etc. Parents also completed questionnaires about the occurrence of imaginary playmates in their children.

For our purposes here it is important to stress that the definition of aggression employed by raters in the present study emphasized overt acts of physical aggression directed towards other children or towards property. Aggressive play behavior in which, for example, two plastic soldiers might be knocked against each other to simulate a battle were not scored as aggressive. Playful "shooting" at each other by children in the course of the make-believe game similarly would not count as aggression. We limited ourselves to direct physical attacks by children against each other, knocking over of other's blocks, pushing, efforts to stamp on a doll or to tear posters off a wall. In general, we did not find high levels of aggressive behavior in our children over the year. Indeed, on the five point scale even our most aggressive children did not average above a score of three except occasionally. Nevertheless, we obtained sufficient variability and also indications of consistency of aggressive behavior in particular children to produce reliable and statistical results.

Variables in the Study

Background and predispositional variables included IQ based on the Peabody Picture Vocabulary Test, the Imagination Interview (Singer, 1973) and the Barron Movement Threshold Inkblot administered to the child as well as the parent's report of the child's imaginary playmates at home. Social class was rated on a five point scale based on the Hollingshead and Redlich criteria. Ethnic Groups was scored on a four point scale in which White was 1, Oriental was 2, Hispanic 3 and Black 4. For correlational purposes we also included sex and age as variables with sex being scored as 1 = female, 2 = male. Observational variables included imaginativeness of play, positive affect, persistence or concentration, aggression, interaction with peers and with adults, and a series of mood ratings such as sadness, anger, fatigue, etc.

The language of the children such as the use of nouns, verbs and other parts of speech, the number of words used during the ten minute observation, the average length of an utterance produced by the child during the ten minute observation and the mean length of utterance were also scored. Particular note was also taken of whether or not references were made to television characters or settings.

The television variables included the Average Number of Hours the child watched TV weekly (based on two week samples in each probe period), and the category of TV watching, e.g., cartoons, commercial children's TV shows (Captain Kangaroo), educational TV children's shows (Misterogers' Neighborhood, Sesame Street), situation-comedies, non-violent family drama (The Waltons), game shows (The Gong Show), action-adventure shows (Starsky & Hutch, Bionic Woman, Emergency).

We also obtained data on whether the child watched alone, with other children or with parents; parents also rated the degree of concentration on the set the child showed during a given viewing period. This latter variable, TV viewing intensity, turned out to be an interesting one because it tended to be negatively associated with the general frequency of TV viewing which the child showed but was positively associated with the degree of persistence the child showed during spontaneous play behavior in nursery school and in general with other measures of imaginativeness and social cooperation in settings outside the home.

Correlational Findings: TV Viewing and Aggression

The first question to be asked in our investigation of the relationship of TV viewing and aggression is whether there is any correlation at all between home viewing and aggressive behavior shown in the nursery school. The answer from our data is clearly a positive one. If we obtain the average scores for TV viewing frequency for the child across the entire year of the study and correlate that with the average aggression score shown by the child over the year (based on 8 independent observations) we find an average correlation of .35 between weekly TV viewing and aggression ($p < .001$). Correlation between the viewing of specifically the Action/Adventure shows and aggression is .33 ($p < .001$). Correlations between viewing of other types of programming and overt aggression are on the whole lower than those for the viewing of the particularly aggressive Action shows and behavioral aggression.

If we divide the sample according to sex, we find that the average correlations for boys are still highly significant and just a few points lower than the average correlation. The results for girls are, however, much more dramatic; for aggression and weekly TV, the correlation is .54 (p<.001) and for aggression and viewing of action shows the correlation is .41 (p<.001).

In general, these correlations are, if anything, higher than those reported in earlier studies with older children.

Another way of approaching this data is to look at the patterns of correlations and the clusterings that emerge across the many different variables of the study. Here we resort to factor analyses of the matrix of intercorrelations between the various background variables, the observed play variables and the language and television viewing variables. The results of one factor analysis (and of the correlations of each measure with the factor) are presented in Table 2. This data is based on a factor analysis with oblique rotation. Essentially comparable results are obtained if orthogonal

TABLE 1

CONTEMPORANEOUS CORRELATIONS OF OVERT AGGRESSION RATINGS
AND TELEVISION VIEWING

Probe Period	Boys	Girls	Total Sample
Aggression with Weekly Total Television Viewing			
February 1977	.32***	.04	.24**
April 1977	.26*	.26*	.30***
October 1977	.03	.68***	.24*
February 1978	.23*	-.21*	.14
Mean Scores Across Four Probes	.31***	.54***	.35***
Aggression with Viewing of Action Shows			
February 1977	.01	-.11	.05
April 1977	.24*	.17	.25**
October 1977	.19*	.64***	.34***
February 1978	.19*	-.01	.18*
Mean Scores Across Four Probes	.32***	.41**	.33***

NOTE: Parent Intervention began in the Spring of 1977 and some of its effects may be influencing results in the October, 1977 and February, 1978 probes.
  *p < .05
  **p < .01
  ***p < .001

TABLE 2. CORRELATIONS OF VARIABLES WITH FACTORS IN OBLIQUE ROTATION

Variable	"Expressive Play" Factor 1	"TV-Viewing and Aggression" Factor 2	"Cooperation, Persistence and Imagination vs. Aggression and Dysphoric Moods" Factor 3
Sex (M = 1, F = 2)	-.32		.26
IQ	.28	-.30	.31
Age			.30
SES (I-V)		.46	
Ethnic Groups (White=1 Black=4)		.21	
Imagination Interview (Home Play)			.35
Barron M. Responses (Imagination)			.28
Imaginary Companion Index			.32
Imaginativeness in Play	.78		.23
Positive Affect	.77		.36
Persistence During Play	.19		.52
Aggression	.27	.51	-.68
Peer Interaction	.82		.28
Peer Cooperation	.56		.56
Fearfulness	-.33		-.45
Anger	.28	.37	-.52
Sadness	-.31		-.50
Fatigue	-.60	-.18	
Liveliness (Motor activity)	.83	.25	
Number of Words	.69		.46
Number of Utterances	.72		.41
Mean Length of Utterance	.34		.50
Future Verbs	.35		.50

TABLE 2. Continued

Variable	"Expressive Play" Factor 1	"TV-Viewing and Aggression" Factor 2	"Cooperation, Persistence and Imagination vs. Aggression and Dysphoric Moods" Factor 3
Weekly TV-Viewing		.97	
TV-Viewing Intensity (Home concentration)		-.17	.24
Cartoons	.22	.76	
Educational TV (Sesame St., Misterogers)			.30
Variety/Game Shows		.70	
Adult Family Drama (Waltons, etc.)		.67	
Action-Adventure (Violent Shows)		.66	-.21

NOTE: Omitted factor loadings are those close to zero.

factor analyses are carried out and also if factor analyses are carried out at each of the four probe periods.
The data presented here represent only the cumulative results over all four probes through the year. It is clear
from the observations of this analysis that Factor 1 represents a kind of General Expressiveness of Play factor which
bears only minimal relationship to the TV viewing patterns
the children show. Factor 2 has its highest loadings for
the TV variables and might at first be considered an instrumental factor except for the fact that Aggression as observed in nursery school .51 on this factor and Anger shown
during play also loads .37 on the factor. It is also apparent that social class loads noticeably on the factor suggesting that we find greater aggressiveness from chidren in
the lower socioeconomic background, a result that might
have been expected based on earlier research. The third
factor clearly represents a kind of social maturity and
imaginativeness factor in which measures of peer cooperation and verbal expressiveness load positively along with
some of the measures of imaginativeness while aggression
and the more negative affective reactions load negatively.
It is worth noting here that of the TV variables, Action
TV tends to load negatively on this third factor while the
viewing of Educational TV shows tends to load positively.
Since these are oblique factors it is possible to extract
second order factors and it is clear that at the second
order level Factors 2 and 3 are inversely related, thus
suggesting that the TV and aggression dimension is negatively
linked to indications of inner imagination and cooperative
behavior in social interaction.

Multiple Regression Analyses

What combinations of variables best predict the likelihood that a child will engage in aggressive behavior in
the nursery school? For if we combine the sexes and look
at the data accumulated over the year, it turns out that the
viewing of Action shows, of News shows and of Game shows
as well as the total amount of weekly TV viewing all combined to be significant predictors of Aggression(R^2=.489,
F=9.3, df=13,127, p <.001). In general, in the attempt to
predict aggression, we find heavy implications of the TV
variables, with Action shows generally near the top in prediction.

Another form of multivariate methodology involves
examination of the relationship between two "domains" of
variables to see if one can find statistically significant
relationships between clusters of variables already shown
to relate to each other. This procedure is called <u>canonical</u>

analysis. Such an analysis (Table 3) from our overall correlation matrix yields one significant canonical variable
(X^2=244.59, df=175, p < .001, eigenvalue=.70, canonical correlation =.84). Of the two domains listed in the table,
one group of variables are clearly the TV log scores including Weekly TV, Cartoons, Variety/Game shows, Adult-oriented
family shows and Action/Adventure programs. The last group
presents the highest loading on this domain. It is interesting to note that intensity of concentration during home
viewing as well as the frequency of watching programs such
as Misterogers' Neighborhood or Sesame Street load negatively on this variable group. On the second set of variables
defining the canonical variate we find aggression, anger,
sadness, gross motor activity and the use of TV references
in spontaneous language as well as socioeconomic status all
loading positively while IQ, fatigue-sluggishness and the
mean length of utterances produced by the child load negatively. Essentially the same results are obtained if we
repeat our analysis omitting the TV frequency of viewing
variables and limit ourselves only to type of programming
for this analysis.

TABLE 3

CANONICAL CORRELATION ANALYSES OF TELEVISION VIEWING
WITH BEHAVIOR AND LANGUAGE VARIABLES

Variable	Loading on First Canonical Variate
Television Variables (Set 1)	
Weekly TV	.78
Cartoons	.69
Variety-Game Shows	.75
Adult Family Dramas	.42
Action-Adventure	.82
TV Intensity (Concentration at home)	−.19
Education TV Children's Shows	−.20
Behavior, Language Variables (Set 2)	
Aggression	.46
Anger	.31
Sadness	.20
Liveliness (Motoric)	.28
TV References	.27
Future Verbs	.26
Socioeconomic Status	.61
Race	.39
IQ	−.22
Fatigue-Sluggishness	−.22
Mean Length of Utterances	−.19

TABLE 4. CONTEMPORANEOUS CORRELATIONS OF AGGRESSION AND TELEVISION VIEWING WHEN DEMOGRAPHIC VARIABLES ARE PARTIALLED OUT (BASED ON MEAN SCORES ACROSS FOUR PROBES FOR TV AND BEHAVIORAL VARIABLES) (N=121)

Variable Pair	Original Correlation	1st, 2nd and 3rd Order Partial Correlations Controlling for:						
		SES	ETHNIC GP.	IQ	SES-ETHNIC	SES-IQ	ETHNIC-IQ	SES-ETHNIC-IQ
School Behavior TV-Viewing								
Total Sample								
Aggression-Weekly TV	.35***	.34***	.32***	.30***	.33***	.30***	.28***	.30***
Aggression-Action Shows	.33***	.31***	.28***	.28***	.29***	.29***	.24***	.25***
Anger-Weekly TV	.24**	.22**	.21**	.22**	.21**	.21**	.19*	.20*
Anger-Action Shows	.20**	.18*	.13	.18*	.13	.16*	.12	.11
Boys								
Aggression-Weekly TV	.31***	.28**	.28**	.22*	.29**	.22*	.22*	.23*
Aggression-Actions Shows	.32***	.29**	.29**	.25*	.30**	.25*	.23*	.24*
Anger-Weekly TV	.24*	.23*	.20	.19	.24*	.21*	.19	.23*
Anger-Action Shows	.32***	.32***	.26*	.28**	.30**	.30**	.25*	.29**
Girls								
Aggression-Weekly TV	.54***	.51***	.53***	.54***	.50***	.52***	.53***	.51***
Aggression-Action Shows	.41***	.34**	.39***	.39***	.35*	.33**	.38***	.34***
Anger-Weekly TV	.25*	.18	.24	.23*	.16	.16	.22*	.15
Anger-Action Shows	.00	-.09	-.04	-.01	-.15	.10	-.07	-.18

***p < .001
**p < .01
*p < .05

In effect, canonical analysis indicates that there is a clear linkage between parents' reports of TV viewing by the child and more "unpleasant" behavioral patterns in the nursery school setting with particular emphasis on the Action-Adventure shows being linked to overt aggression. It is also clear that children who make much reference to television in their spontaneous activities line up on this canonical variant while children who talk a great deal without necessarily referring to TV tend to load negatively on the behavior dimension linked to television viewing.

Partial Correlational Analysis

Social class and general intelligence (as estimated by the Peabody Picture Vocabulary Test) do indeed show relationships to TV viewing. Is our finding of a link between aggression and the watching of a great deal of TV or of action shows simply a consequence of intelligence, social class or possibly even ethnic differences in viewing patterns as well as in aggression? To rule out the possibility that our findings merely reflect class or intelligence group viewing and behavioral styles we carried out a series of systematic partial correlation analyses. These are presented in Table 4. Inspection of this table indicates quite clearly that even when we partial out either individually or together the effects of socioeconomic status, ethnicity and IQ, correlations between aggression and weekly TV viewing or aggression and the viewing of Action/Adventure shows are still significant. This is particularly evident for girls; for boys there is some drop in the overall magnitude of the original correlations but significant relationships still emerge. Social class, ethnic status and IQ cannot alone or in combination account for the persisting correlations between observed aggressive behavior in the children and reports of their home viewing patterns of TV.

Cross-Lag Correlational Patterns

We still have at best indicated only covariation of aggression and TV viewing. The question might be raised that it is just as likely that highly aggressive children choose to watch a lot of television or a lot of Action/Adventure shows as to argue that the direction of causality flows from viewing towards overt behavior. It might, of course, also be maintained that the search for simple causality is a fruitless one and that the growth patterns of three- and four-year-olds are complexly determined.

One way at least to eliminate certain explanations is to look at correlations over time. Suppose the fre-

quency of TV viewing is itself more likely to be brought
about by the fact that children who are already aggressive
are attracted to the TV set. Then we should expect that
correlations between aggression at earlier times and the TV
measures _later_ in the year would generally run higher than
those for TV viewing early in the year and aggression later
in the year. Table 5 provides the necessary data broken
down for total sample and for the boys and girls.

If it is initial aggression which produces later TV
viewing patterns, e.g. for Action/Adventure shows, then we
should get high correlations between aggression in the earlier probes such as 1 and 2 and later TV viewing. It is
clear, however, from this table that in the initial probes
the correlations between aggression at Time 1 and Action/
Adventure viewing at Time 2 or Time 3 are non-significant
while those for Action/Adventure TV viewing at Probe 1 and
aggression at Times 2 and 3 are statistically significant.

Subsequently, during the year, there are, however,
reversals of this direction but the overall pattern of data

TABLE 5

CORRELATIONS BETWEEN ACTION SHOW VIEWING AND SUBSEQUENT
OR PRIOR BEHAVIORAL AGGRESSION RATINGS

Mean Hours Watching Action Shows Probe	Overt Aggression Probe	Total Sample	Sample	
			Boys	Girls
1	2	.33***	.27**	.32**
1	3	.35***	.28**	.40***
1	4	.16	.15	.19
2	3	.22**	.19*	.24*
2	4	.08	-.02	.29*
3	4	.26**	.28**	.15
2	1	.08	.12	-.14
3	1	.04	.03	.10
4	1	.09	.11	-.14
3	2	.20*	.11	.23*
4	2	.28*	.24*	.33**
4	3	.43*	.41***	.40***

NOTE: Ns on which correlations are based may vary from
group to group, thereby accounting for differing
significance levels for similar correlation coef-
ficients.
   *p < .05
  **p < .01
 ***p < .001

certainly rules out the easy explanation that aggressive children prefer Action TV shows and that this preferential viewing tendency is sufficient to explain our correlations. If anything, a careful examination of the pattern of Cross-Lag Correlations seems to support the notion that earlier in the year the TV viewing patterns are much more likely related to later aggressive behavior.

In effect, our Cross-Lag Correlations do not conclusively implicate TV viewing as an exclusive causal factor in producing later aggressive behavior. Nevertheless, they seem on the whole to rule out the explanation that it is simply a preferential pattern we are observing with aggressive children generally electing to watch Action/Adventure shows. If anything, the trend does suggest that it is the TV viewing pattern which is more likely to be linked to later aggressive behavior.

This point is made in another way if we divide our subjects into extreme groups, those who show initially minimum TV viewing and minimum aggression or those who show initially heavy TV viewing and somewhat higher levels of aggression in the first probe. If we then plot subsequent increases in aggressive behavior we find, as can be seen in Table 6, that the greatest increases in aggression emerge for those children who are initially either low in aggression or high in aggression but who are in both cases high in television viewing compared to the total sample. While the children who are low TV viewers and initially high aggression also show an increase in aggression, this result emerges only by the time of the fourth probe. Those children who are initially low in TV viewing and low in aggression show only a very slight increase in aggressive behavior over the year.

It is important to note that we have obtained comparable results from girls as well as from boys. The study by Lefkowitz et al. (1977) had found TV-aggression correlation results only for boys and, in general, earlier studies had also reported the stronger results for boys than for girls. Our data, even though based on a much smaller number of girls who actually show aggressive acts, nevertheless reflects positive relationships between aggression and TV viewing for girls. Indeed, these results for girls are even stronger in our study than for boys. One should keep in mind during the past couple of years there has been a marked increase in the availability on TV of female "superheroines", Wonder Woman, Bionic Woman, Isis, Charlie's Angels, all of whom represent female models who themselves engage in aggressive acts. It is hard to avoid the conclusion from our data that TV viewing by children of three and four does

TABLE 6. MEANS OF PHYSICAL AGGRESSION ON LATER PROBES BASED ON EXTREME SAMPLES INITIAL (PROBE 1) AGGRESSION OF AND WEEKLY TV-VIEWING FOR BOYS (Probe 1)

Variable Aggression	Low Television Low Aggression	High Television Low Aggression	Low Television High Aggression	High Television High Aggression
Aggression, Probe 1	1.0	1.0	1.4	1.4
Aggression, Probe 2	1.1	1.4	1.4	1.4
Aggression, Probe 3	1.4	1.5	1.2	2.2
Aggression, Probe 4	1.4	1.9	2.1	2.0
	(N=24)	(N=7)	(N=10)	(N=5)

play an important part in the likelihood that they will show
aggressive behavior with adults in the course of nursery
school activity.

Family Interview Study

Objectives of Family Interviews

In looking for the "smoking gun" that might link TV
viewing to specific aggression shown at school, it seems
desirable to try to look more closely at home life patterns
of the children in our study. Even though our data indicate
that gross measurements of family background such as ethnicity and social class cannot account for the link between
TV viewing and aggression, it remains possible that there
are more specific factors within family settings that might
determine this correlation. For example, it is entirely
possible that children who watch a lot of television and
also show a good deal of aggression can come from homes that
are characterized by considerable family fighting, disor-
ganization, psychological or economic stress, etc. In such
a case it could be argued that heavy TV viewing or even
preference for action shows and the occurrence of aggression
in the child both reflect reactions to a common family emphasis on violence or to a traumatic, disorganized family life.

Our strategy was to identify four groups of children
who represented the extremes in both TV viewing and aggression for our total sample. Thus, we were able to select
ten children who could be identified over the year as high
in TV viewing and high in behavioral aggression, ten children who were low in TV viewing and also high in behavioral
aggression, ten children who were high TV viewers but showed
relatively little overt aggression and finally ten children
who were low both in TV viewing and aggression over the year.
Each of the groups consisted of six boys and four girls.
The groups were selected on the basis of their final total
scores being above or below the sample median on the relevant variables and also on the basis of their scores being
above or below the sample medians on at least three of the
four trimonthly probes. Thus, we had fairly clear-cut extremes numbering somewhat less than a third of our total
sample.

The rationale for the choice of these extremes is as
follows. If there is a major family mediating variable such
as the occurrence of aggression in the family that is critical we should find essentially no difference between the two
high aggressive groups who differ only in frequency of their
TV viewing patterns. Both of these groups should differ

markedly from the low aggression group by reflecting more
family fighting, more parental conflict, more disruptive
familial situations, evidence of stresses and bereavements
in the family life, perhaps even broken families or other
home situations that have generally been found linked to
overt aggressive behavior in older children. If, on the
other hand, for this sample, the role of television plays a
more <u>causal</u> role in the occurrences of aggressive behavior,
then we might expect that our high TV-high aggression families may not differ very much from families who are low TV
viewers with little aggression or from high TV viewers with
little aggression. In other words, we ought to find no
clear-cut evidence of unique family factors that model aggression. Instead, perhaps, we may expect to find a laxity
in control by parents over TV viewing of violent programming
or other highly arousing material. The low TV but high aggressive group ought, however, to show some signs of aggressive modeling by parents or at least of disruption and diffi-
culty so as to yield some clue as to why aggression should
occur in the absence of heavy TV viewing.

We still are left with the question about why high TV
viewers who do not score above the group median on aggression should not seem to be aggressive. Here we must consider the possibility that there may be factors in the pattern
of TV viewing itself for these subjects and in the patterns
of family attitude or in the imaginative style of the child
which would operate to <u>mitigate</u> the potentially noxious
influences of the television viewing patterns.

A special advantage of looking into the home life of
the children also affords us a chance to verify some of the
findings we have obtained from the regular parental log keeping and also from our observations in the nursery school.
To what extent does it turn out that parents in direct
interview report much the same frequency of TV viewing as we
obtained from their log-keeping records? To what extent are
children who are observed to be aggressive in the nursery
school are so reported by their parents in their behavior
at home? The reader should keep in mind that our interviewers as well as the parents did not know what groups
their children fell into on the basis of the scoring of TV
logs or of the behavioral variables. Thus, any consistencies which emerged can only be attributed to consistencies
demonstrated by the child itself in different settings.

Procedures

In preparing our questionnaires for use with the parents we tried to take into account the structural charac-

teristics of the home, its orderliness, neatness, the availability of weapons (such as gun racks hanging on the wall), the indications of regular daily routines for parents and children, etc. Parents were encouraged to describe in detail the day-to-day wake-up, mealtime, recreational and sleep patterns of both parents and children. Indications of difficulties in the home ranging from parental disagreements, sibling disagreements, economic and emotional stresses, bereavements, family illnesses, parental separations, etc., were explored. Family television viewing patterns were also queried at considerable length. Evidence of emotional disturbance or patterns of distress in the children were also looked for in the replies of the parents about the children's health and general well-being.

We were particularly interested in obtaining evidence not only of disturbances but of possible strengths in the family life or specifically in the child's behavior. We considered it likely that parental emphasis on story-telling, reading, and imaginative stimulation might provide the child with alternative forms of play and operate against the child's direct imitation of aggressive material witnessed on television. We felt that this broader behavioral repertory would reduce the chances that aggression would be a preferred or highly valued, perhaps because of over-learning, method of coping with frustration or stress. Goldberg (1973) had reported that children who showed evidence of greater imagination were less likely to be aggressive than those who showed a paucity of fantasy in their repertory of reactions.

Results of Family Interviews

Family interviews lasted between ninety minutes and two hours generally. Mothers were extremely cooperative and talked willingly, indeed almost eagerly, about a tremendous range of details of family life. Thus, it was often possible for interviewers to score particular variables without even having to ask specific questions from the interview schedule.

Statistical tests were carried out on more than 30 items reflecting issues involving the daily routines, patterns of family discipline, leisure activities and TV viewing habits of each of the families. Perhaps the most striking outcome of the interview study are the indications that the families differed only on a relatively small number of variables. In effect we find greater commonalities across the four types of families than differences between them. Thus, gross differences which might be expected to account

for aggression such as evidence of family disputes, reports
of violent or aggressive emphases in the home, indications
of great family stress or disruption do not emerge predominantly in one or another group. Perhaps a third of the
families in this sample were undergoing periods of marital
breakup or other types of stress such as recent bereavement.
These problems were spread across the four subgroups, however, and did not predominate in any one of them.

In general, therefore, it does not seem reasonable to
interpret the origins of aggression in these preschoolers
as a consequence of any clear indications of gross modeling
of family violence or as reactions to clear evidence of turmoil in family life. It is worth noting, however, that one
group does stand out from the other three in relation to a
series of statistical differences that are worth examining.
This group is the high aggressive, high television viewing
group. The families of these children are characterized by
a considerable laxity in control of the television on the
part of the parents and in general of a very limited range
of outside interests and activities manifested by the family group. In other words, the children who are the high
viewers and who also show more aggressive behavior in the
nursery school seem to come from families in which, as the
mothers clearly indicate, the child essentially controls
his or her own TV watching time. There is no countervailing force provided by other family interests such as in
music, reading, outdoor recreation, arts or crafts, etc.
The impression presented is therefore one of family style
in which television-viewing becomes a major focus of family
life and recreation.

Let us take a closer look at the profiles of the
families as they emerged. Here, where possible, we will
indicate those variables in which statistically reliable
differences emerged for the four groups particularly indicating a deviation of the specific family types from the
other families.

High TV Watching-High Aggression

The children in our high aggressive and high television viewing group turn out to be significantly lower in
their IQ scores than the children in the other groups (p<
.002). As a matter of fact, both high television-watch-
ing groups are significantly lower in IQ than the 2 groups
that are rated as low frequency viewers, but the high TV-
high aggression groups with an average IQ of 104 is clearly
the lowest. The high viewers in general are from families

of somewhat lower socioeconomic status than low viewers. Nevertheless, one cannot attribute the aggression of the child to the intelligence differences or a social class difference since the high television-low aggression group clearly does not show much aggression initially. The social class difference seems rather to be much more linked to the tendency simply to watch more television (p < .001).

Interviewers rated the homes of both high aggression groups as somewhat more disorganized than that of the other families. Of particular importance in the high television-high aggression group was the fact that there were fewer toys in evidence around the home and by far the least evidence of books (p < .0007) and of musical instruments or records (p < .05). Children in this group tended to be allowed to stay up later at night. They also woke up later in the morning than the children in the other groups. Indeed, their fathers' patterns also reflected tendencies to wake up later in the morning both on weekdays and weekends (p < .03, p < .07) than the fathers in the other groups. In general, the high aggressive, high TV viewing families seemed to reflect a somewhat more conventional male-female relationship with the father showing less interest in homemaking activities than do the fathers in the other groups (p < .02).

What seems to stand out more clearly than anything else for the high television-high aggressive child's life style is a gross laxity of control by parents of the TV viewing situation in the home. These families even report themselves to be generally more likely to watch television while they eat. As might be expected from the television data, the mothers report in the interviews as well that children from the high TV viewing groups spend more time watching television both in the morning and at night. The children in this group are allowed to stay up later (p < .04), they are less likely to have a bedtime routine (p < .07), they are less likely to have stories told to them at bedtime (p=.02), and they are less likely to have a kind of calming down period before going to bed (p=.09).

Thus, we see a pattern in which the child on awakening in the morning starts out with the TV, picks it up on return from nursery school and later joined apparently by the family goes on to watch until relatively late at night when he or she is trundled off to bed without much verbal interchange or a quieting period. The conventionality of these families is further stressed by the fact that this group is the one which stands out significantly from the others

in requiring children to say a prayer before bedtime
(p < .008). For three- and four-year-olds a prayer is per-
functory at best and certainly quite different from the
slow easing into bedtime described by the other families in
which there is a story-time and some type of parent-child
interchange. Again, the issue to be stressed is that on
the specific item of who controls the TV set, it is the
high TV-high aggression group mothers who report that it is
the child who controls the television set in their homes
(p=.007).

In keeping with the limited range of interest we have
mentioned, a closer look at the specific patterns for the
high television-high aggression child's family suggests a
minimum of outside interests. In contrast with other groups
with children who are often taken to parks, picnics, museums
or other cultural activities, the child in this group is most
likely to spend time with parents going shopping. The
only other outside recreation reported is trips to the movies
with parents. Thus, the influence of the popular media and
of the potentially arousing or violent components of movies
or TV are further emphasized by the nature of the family
activities with the children. This point is further emphasized by indications of trends toward differences in parental
tastes about TV fare. The fathers of this group are reported
as showing more interest in team sports emphasizing body
contact or aggressive activity such as hockey and football.
The fathers generally watch this type of fare on TV with the
child.

The mothers' reports confirm what we have observed
about the children in the nursery school. For both high
aggressive groups there is greater evidence of argument
occurring between children in the family. Mothers described
the high aggressive children from both TV watching groups
as showing greater emphasis on physical versus verbal fighting. It is an important confirmation of our nursery school
data and suggests consistency from home to nursery school
in the aggressive tendencies of the children.

In our search for the origins of aggression what can
we say about this special characteristic of the family life
of both high aggressive groups irrespective of the amount of
television watching? It is certainly true that children of
both high aggressive groups are more likely to be punished
by spanking according to reports by the mothers (p=.08).
Mothers also report significantly more often that the child
is unlikely to be rewarded by praise (p=.01). What is not
clear of course is whether the fact that the children are

already somewhat more aggressive brings upon them this reaction from parents or whether it is the parents' use of physical force that establishes a tone. Probably there is a subtle interaction effect in evidence. It is interesting that the high aggressive children are reported in general by their mothers as less likely to show humor and laughter in their day-to-day patterns of behavior. This result in general is in accord with our own findings that positive affect in nursery school, smiling, laughing and intense interest tend to be negatively related to overt aggressive behavior.

High Aggression but Low TV Watching

What differences can we identify between the family styles of the children who are identified as aggressive in the nursery school but who differ drastically in amount of TV viewing? One of the most obvious things that emerges is that the high aggressive but low TV watching children are actually the most intelligent in our sample (an average IQ of 125). Descriptions of the family life patterns seem to reflect the fact that more often in this group both parents are intellectually gifted and professionally active. Family styles themselves indicate a considerable range of interests both cultural and intellectual for both parents. The mothers describe the families as extremely active and autonomous. Indeed, the interviewers who rated the descriptions by the mothers of family life as indicating that this family showed "highest activity level", "most competition", and the most "autonomy" and were the most disorderly in daily routines. Thus the families of these high aggressive but low TV watching children seem to reflect a good deal of self-directed, varied activities by parents that preclude in the hustle and bustle of their lives much watching of television by the children. In this low TV orientation it is worth noting, however, that the children do watch a higher proportion of action-detective shows than do the low aggressive children. It is conceivable, therefore, that these somewhat active, competitive families, apparently on the move in various directions, provide considerable cultural stimulation for their children, minimize TV viewing, but do not prevent the child's watching of the potentially more violent shows. We cannot absolutely assert that this greater activity level in the family is a true modeling of aggressive behavior, but it may create an arousing trend and a greater sense of conflict in the child that then is manifested in greater aggressive behavior in the nursery school setting. It is important to keep in mind here that these children are the brightest in our sample so we cannot attribute aggression only to limited intellectual capacities.

High TV Without Aggression

What then are we to make of the children who are high
TV viewers but low in aggression? Our interviewers characterized the homes of this group as perhaps the most orderly
and organized of all. These children also seemed to stem
from families in which there was a wide range of cultural
activity. If one also examines the pattern of TV viewing,
the group turns out to be watching relatively less of the
action-adventure and violent shows and relatively more than
any other group of the educational or public television shows
such as <u>Misterogers' Neighborhood</u> and <u>Sesame Street</u>. On
tests of imaginativeness, this group clearly scores highest.
In other words, what we seem to see is a pattern in which
parents while allowing the child considerable freedom in
watching television a good deal do seem to have provided
some countervailing influence in the way of cultural interests and encouragement towards the viewing of the more
benign TV fare. The children in this group also seem to be
the most imaginative and therefore may be in a position to
limit the more direct influence of what they watch and instead translate it into fantasy and make-believe games.
There is a considerable body of evidence that suggests that
imaginativeness as measured by response to the Rorschach
Inkblots is consistently negatively related to tendencies
to be overtly aggressive or impulsive.

Conclusions and Implications

Our exploration of the relationship of television to
aggression in preschoolers has still not come up with the
kind of "smoking gun" evidence that might satisfy the se-
verest critics of television research and certainly the
most enthusiastic supporters of the television industry.
We have not found a clear indication of what produces aggression in our preschoolers. At the same time, it seems
as if at least in our study of 40 families representing
the extremes of television viewing and aggression in the
child's nursery school behavior it is possible to rule out
many other proposed explanations. It does not seem from
our data reasonable to assume that children who watch a great
deal of television and who also show aggression in the nursery school do so because of a generally disorderly and
stressful family life. We cannot implicate violent behavior on the part of the parents in explaining the beginnings
of aggression in our relatively normal and on the whole
non-violent samples of preschoolers.

The one factor that stands out most consistently is
that laxity of family control around the TV set and oppor-

tunities for the children to watch the more action oriented
shows are continually linked to the likelihood that the child
will show aggressive behavior at home (according to parents'
reports) and in the nursery school. Our high television-
high aggressive children come from families that are essentially lower middle-class, convential in sex role orientation, traditional in respect to values and relatively limited
with respect to range of cultural interests. For this group
more than any of our others the television medium seems like
a major source of input into consciousness and general orientation of the child. The aggression shown by the children
who are characterized as low TV viewers relative to our
sample seems somewhat more explicable as a response to a
very high pitch of activity in family life in a setting
in which both parents tend to be professionals and to be
"on the go", competitive and autonomous. We can see the
possibility that a general arousal factor rather than specific modeling of aggression may account for some of the disruptive behavior these children show.

A look at the families of the high TV watching, low aggression children suggests that sheer frequency of viewing
is not in itself perhaps the critical factor in generating
the likelihood of aggressive behavior at school. These children while watching a great deal of all kinds of television
show a relatively greater proportion of viewing programming
which we know from other research to have beneficial effects
on children, shows like Misterogers' Neighborhood and Sesame
Street which emphasize prosocial values and cognitive skill
development. They watch a good deal of action shows, of
course, but relatively less even in proportion to the amount
of watching than do those children who are characterized
as low viewers but who show a great deal more aggression
in the nursery school. It is of interest, however, to
notice that for our high TV viewers who are on the whole
lower in aggression there is over the year a fairly sharp
increase in aggression compared with the findings for our
sample of children who are low both in aggression and in
frequency of television viewing.

Let us again remind our readers that our sample of
children are on the whole not grossly violent or aggressive preschoolers. Nevertheless, within this restricted
range of aggressive behavior our data are consistent and
it seems to us rather telling. There is a continuous
link of TV viewing to the likelihood that a child will be
aggressive at the nursery school. The implications of this
finding suggest a number of thoughts with which we will
conclude.

First of all, there seems to be in this material a
message to the television industry. The TV medium for better or worse is accessible to huge numbers of extremely sug-
gestable preschoolers. For many of them, it becomes a
"window on the world" or a "member of the family". Thus
for this medium, even allowing the best intentions of ar-
tistic creativity, it seems that a good deal of self-restraint is called for in programming. We do not mean to suggest that action and violence ought to be eliminated from
the medium. Rather, self-restraint should dictate that
scenes of violence that are relatively easily imitated and
that are relatively easily comprehended by young children
ought to be eliminated wherever possible. The Greek dramas
were full of violence, but it was kept offstage and yet
these plays still have considerable power when performed
today. It is also possible that stylized violence when
necessary to the plot or action and violence in settings
remote from day-to-day reality may have little direct impact
on children. These are researchable questions. It is clear,
however, that we need much more serious thought on the part
of producers and writers about how to present issues on television without relying on the cliché "punchout", car chase
and other forms of arousing situations that might have unfortunate effects on what is essentially a family medium.
Recent reductions of aggressive content on prime-time TV
and modifications in networks' own "self-censorship" codes
reflect a growing awareness of this responsibility by the
industry.

The industry also has, we believe, an obligation to
provide a much greater range of fare for children. The
vast profits made from commercials directed to children could
be applied to producing a higher quality programming including many programs which have already been shown to have use-
ful effects for children. Programs that stimulate imaginative play, that encourage sharing, cooperation, that emphasize values of helping and friendliness would be a tremendous use to preschoolers. The availability of kindly parental or avuncular figures who could communicate directly
with preschoolers and give them some sense of trust and
belonging (perhaps often in the fact of contrary experiences at home) might be much more valuable experience and
might counteract some of the more negative potential of
the medium.

Ultimately, of course, the responsibility for control-
ling the effects of the medium on children rests with parents. It is clear to us from our interviews that the major
differences between the children who watch large amounts of
television but who also differ in their degree of aggres-

sion is the fact that in the case of the aggressive children,
their parents show a complete lack of responsibility concerning what the children watch. They clearly indicate that
they allow the child to determine what is on the TV set. By
contrast, the parents of the children who are high in TV
watching but low in aggression seem to be less involved with
the amount of watching but do seem to play a more active role
in steering the children towards "better types" of programming. They also differ in that they are more willing to spend
time talking with their children, reading stories to them
and providing them with a quiet time before bed. Ultimately,
we cannot escape the fundamental role of the parent as a
source of stability in the child's life, as an influence on
imagination and inner control. There is little doubt that
television in the home is a delightful source of entertain-
ment and a refuge from other cares for parents and children. But we prefer for the growing child the image of a
quiet moment at bedtime when an adult sits by the child's
side and tells a story or reads from a book in a way that
forces the child to stretch its own imagination amid warm
surroundings. Herein we feel lies the best basis for developing a sense of trust and at the same time a broader
ability for private creativity.

References

Bailyn, L. Mass media and children: A study of exposure
habits and cognitive effects. Psychological Monographs,
1959, 73, (1, Whole No. 471).

Bandura, A. Psychological modeling: Conflicting theories.
Chicago: Aldine-Atherton, 1971.

Bandura, A. Aggression: A social learning analysis. Engle-
wood Cliffs, N.J.: Prentice-Hall, 1973.

Bandura, A. The self system in reciprocal determinism.
American Psychologist, 1978, 11, 344-358.

Baron, R.A. Human aggression. New York: Plenum, 1977.

Belson, W.A. Television and the adolescent boy. Hampshire,
England: Saxon House, 1978.

Chaffee, S. Television and adolescent aggressiveness. In
G.A. Comstock & E.A. Rubinstein (Eds.), Television and
social behavior (Vol. 3). Washington, D.C.: Government
Printing Office, 1972.

Cline, V.B., Croft, R.G., & Courrier, S. Desensitization
of children to television violence. Journal of Personality and Social Psychology, 1973, 27, 360-365.

Friedrich, L., & Stein, A. Aggressive and prosocial television programs and the natural behavior of preschool
children. Monographs of the Society for Research in
Child Development, 1973, 38 (4, Serial No. 151).

Goldberg, L. Aggression in boys in a clinic population.
Unpublished doctoral dissertation, City University of
New York, 1973.

Graham, H.D., & Gurr, T.R. (Eds.). The history of violence
in America. New York: Bantam Books, 1969.

Lefkowitz, M.M., Eron, L.D., Walder, L.O., & Huesmann, L.R.
Growing up to be violent. New York: Pergamon, 1977.

McCord, W., McCord, J., & Howard, A. Familial correlates
of aggression in nondelinquent male children. Journal
of Abnormal and Social Psychology, 1969, 62, 79-93.

Murray, J.P., Rubinstein, E.A., & Comstock, G.A. (Eds.). Television and social behavior (Vol. 2). Washington, D.C.: Government Printing Office, 1972.

Noble, G. Film-mediated creative and aggressive play. British Journal of Social and Clinical Psychology, 1970, 9, 1-7.

Noble, G. Effects of different forms of filmed aggression on children's constructive and destructive play. Journal of Personality and Social Psychology, 1973, 26, 54-59.

Noble, G. Children in front of the small screen. London: Constable, 1975.

Schramm, W., Lyle, J., & Parker, E.B. Television in the lives of our children. Stanford, California: Standard University Press, 1961.

Singer, J.L. The child's world of make-believe: Experimental studies of imaginative play. New York: Academic Press, 1973.

Singer, J.L., & Singer, D.G. A member of the family. Yale Alumni Magazine, 1975, 38, 10-15.

Tannenbaum, P.H., & Zillmann. Emotion arousal in the facilitation of aggression through communication. Advances in Experimental Social Psychology, 1975, 8, 149-192.

Watt, J.H., & Krull, R. An examination of three models of television viewing and aggression. Human Communications Research, 1977, 3(2), 99-112.

Discussion:
Television Violence
and the Family

American commercial television has earned its dubious
right to be included in a symposium on family violence--it
is one more contributor to a great social problem. There
has been resistance on the part of the public to recognize
television as anything other than entertainment, and all of
the research by social scientists has yet to have a significant impact on the television industry or on policy making.
The issue of how to cope with a violent socialization agent
in our midst is unreconciled, and very little attention has
been given to ways in which families can learn to recognize,
control or modify the impact of television. In my discussion, I should like to document briefly these rather
gloomy assertions as well as note some remedial steps which
might be taken to help children and families live with
television.

Learning Violence

Since the advent of television in the 1950's, there has
been concern over the changes which this medium might bring
about in family life (Himmelweit, Lyle & Vince, 1958;
Schramm, Lyle & Parker, 1964). The early studies did not
demonstrate dramatic shifts in life styles as families
acquired television sets, but they did reveal that television
had become an integral part of the family. The next major
focus of concern was television content, specifically
violent content, and whether or not it contributes to rising
crime rates and real-life violence. Periodic congressional
bouts over this question ultimately culminated in the
Surgeon-General's research program in the early 1970's
(1972). The five volumes of technical papers which appeared
in 1972 present a formidable picture. First, over 90% of
American families had television sets in their homes and
children were averaging 2-4 hours of daily viewing--or

spending more time watching TV than any single activity except sleeping. Second, content analyses by Gerbner showed the violent-saturated nature of American television, particularly childrens' television. Third, children were learning from television--from laboratory, field and correlational studies, the convergent evidence was that viewing of television violence is related to aggressive attitudes and serves to reduce self-control and tolerance of frustration and instigate aggressive behavior (Stein & Friedrich, 1975; Surgeon-General's Scientific Advisory Committee, 1972).

The research reported by the Singers today again affirms the contribution of violent television watching to aggressive behaviors with peers and within the family. It is also worth noting that they, as earlier researchers, have found that the correlation between violent viewing and aggression cannot be accounted for by other auspicious variable such as social class, I.Q., parental aggression, parental warmth, parental viewing of television or styles of family communication (Stein & Friedrich, 1975). While some yet-to-be-discovered third variable may account for the relationship, the evidence strongly suggests that this correlation is not due to a third variable.

Individual Differences

So we are left with the uneasy knowledge that televised violence can, and to some unknown extent does, promote aggressive attitudes and behavior in children and adolescents. Further, we have some information about individual differences in children and family life styles which point to what might be called "high risk" viewers of television. First, let us consider some individual differences in responses to violent television. One fairly clear finding from the Surgeon-General's program research was that television violence had a greater effect on the more aggressive children and adolescents (Friedrich & Stein, 1973; Parke, et al., 1974; Robinson & Bachman, 1972; Steur, et al., 1971; Wells, 1973). While the effects are not limited to this group, as I have already stated, they are more pronounced. Nor am I referring to some deviant minority--they are frequently a rather large segment of the samples studied. While above average in aggression, they are definitely within the "normal range". Further, the person who is angry or frustrated may be particularly attentive to film violence and more likely to imitate it (Berkowitz, 1970; Goranson, 1970).

Family Differences

Now, let us turn to the scattered findings on families. Children from lower-social-status families watch more television and watch more violence than those from higher status homes. Blacks also watch more television and more violent television than whites, even when social status is controlled (Lyle, 1972). Children's viewing of violent programs is related to their parents' viewing of similar programs (Chaffee & McLeod, 1972; Friedrich & Stein, 1973; Greenberg, Ericson & Vlahos, 1972; Lyle & Hoffman, 1972; McLeod, Atkin & Chaffee, 1972). Thus, those children and those families who are most aggressive, and most under societal and economic stress both seek out and respond most to aggressive television.

Social Isolation

Another source of stress which has been mentioned frequently in this symposium is social isolation and lack of contact with supportive family and friends. In this context, I find the Singers' interviews with high aggressive-high TV families most interesting. It seems that for these families the total laxity of parental control over television is accompanied by a dirth of outside interests, activities, and social contacts. Television becomes the major focus of family life and recreation. While for all children television may contribute to their learning and knowledge of social norms and views of behavior that is rewarded and successful, for some children it may become a far more important socializing influence.

Television and Sex

Thus far, I have limited my discussion to the issue of violent television content and its potential contribution to aggressive attitudes and behavior. However, there are other negative aspects of commercial television content which have received less attention and are worthy of mention: the increasing amount of explicit sex and sex combined with violence, the verbal and psychological abuse which is stock and trade of the popular "family hour" comedy shows; the stereotypic portrayals of females, the elderly, minority group members; and the parade of affluence (with almost no work portrayed) coupled with the endless barrage of ads for expensive toys and material goods. If children and families rely upon television as the "window to the world", especially if they are poor and minority group members, the view is a bleak and frustrating one.

Paucity of Constructive Television

Another quite different limitation of the discussion thus far is the omission of television programming which has potential to contribute to the positive development of intellectual and social skills. "Sesame Street" has a unique place in American television history. Its first claim to fame is that the program is the result of a long and continuously evolving effort by a group of social scientists, writers and producers (Lesser, 1974). They have succeeded in producing a program which appeals to children of all socioeconomic classes. Further, it has not only been an economic success, but research evaluations document that children can learn important cognitive skills by watching the program (Ball & Bogatz, 1970; Bogatz & Ball, 1971). There is also some evidence that long-term viewers acquire more positive attitudes toward members of other racial groups (Bogatz & Ball, 1971). Another program designed for preschool children is also unique for a somewhat different set of reasons. "Mr. Rogers' Neighborhood" is the product of the creative efforts of psychologists and the writer-producer, Fred Rogers. The emphasis of the program is social and emotional development of young children, particularly young children and the family. My colleague, Aletha Stein, and I conducted a series of studies in which children saw this program in natural settings, such as the nursery school, and in laboratory settings. We found that young children could learn complex prosocial messages from the program and showed increases in self-control as well as increases in positive interpersonal behaviors with their peers after viewing it (Friedrich & Stein, 1973; Friedrich & Stein, 1975; Friedrich et al., 1975). So there is evidence that children can learn constructive as well as destructive messages from television. However, it is also clear that a great deal more research is necessary before we know how to present educational and prosocial content in effective ways. A promising new focus of research is concerned with production techniques--both audio and visual-- which may influence attention and learning of program content (Huston-Stein, 1978). Violent, arousing content is simple to learn and relatively easy to express given the everyday frustrations of life within the family. But learning to cooperate, to tolerate disappointments and frustrations and to control feelings is far more complex. Moreover, we know relatively little about children's learning of prosocial content and we know even less about the ways in which families use educational television. From studies in America and Israel it has been found that encouraging mothers to watch "Sesame Street" with their children and talk about it with them made a large contribution to the amount of viewing

of disadvantaged children and the amount they learn from
the program (Ball & Bogatz, 1970; Salomon, 1973). Viewing
with the mother resulted in higher gains for children from
a lower socioeconomic group than from a middle socioeconomic
group. Unfortunately, we have no data on family viewing
and discussion of other educational or "prosocial" programs.

Problems of Government Action

The most modest statement one can make in reviewing the
current status of our knowledge and lack of knowledge about
television is that we ought to be able to do something to
improve programming and to make television a more positive
influence on family life than it is now. While this sounds
simple enough, the problems we face are enormous, and do
not lend themselves well to fast solutions. Specific policy
recommendations did not flow from the Surgeon-General's
program of research and there is no automatic step from
social science research to public policy (Rubinstein, 1978).
Despite the Surgeon-General, Jesse Steinfeld's statement
that "these studies make it clear to me that the relationship between televised violence and antisocial behavior is
sufficiently proved to warrant immediate remedial action,"
(Steinfeld, 1973) there has been no government action.
While it would be naive to have assumed sweeping regulatory
changes would emerge, it is rather striking that John
Pastore's request to the Secretary of HEW and the FCC for
the publication of an annual violence index has not been
acted upon (Rubinstein, 1978).

Community Action

Remedial action has also been sought by public interest
groups employing a variety of tactics. Action for Childrens'
Television began with an energetic campaign of criticism
against television fare and advertising practices, but has
expanded efforts to include providing forums in which
researchers, writers and producers and network representatives can discuss programming. The Council for Children,
Media and Merchandising has long been active in lobbying
for children's interests in advertising practices. In
addition, the advocacy group headed by former FCC Commis-
sioner, Nicholas Johnson, the National Citizen's Committee
for Broadcasting, employed a firm to monitor commercials
and programs and provides an annual report identifying the
sponsors of the most violent programs. In 1976, the American Medical Association, the American Psychiatric Association and the National Parent-Teacher Association inaugurated
campaigns against television violence.

However, criticism and debate seem to have reaped us few rewards. While some decrease occurred in television violence during the 1977-78 season, the decline as measured by Gerbner's annual index from 1969-1977 was negligible (Gerbner et al., 1978). There have been some efforts made to improve the quality of childrens' programming, but one can still point to the few exceptions in the familiar parade. It would be naive to assume sweeping industry self-reform could take place given the economic reliance upon popular ratings. Swift or radical moves could mean financial disaster for a network. But industry, like government, can be faulted for failing to recognize and act upon the need for intensive and long-term planning to improve the quality of programming. There now exists no funding from either the government or networks for the sort of research program which is necessary to develop guidelines for television production. Eli Rubinstein, among others, has repeatedly proposed the funding of a major long-term program of research. He points out that with the American television industry operating at about a $10 billion dollar annual budget, even 1/10 of one percent devoted to social research would amount to $10 million dollars a year (Rubinstein, 1978). If such a budget were supplemented by other public and private sources, we might in time know better how to live with television and how to give humanistic direction to this form of technology.

Models from Europe

It is obvious by now that I am focusing on long-term goals involving the active participation of social scien-tists, private foundations, government, industry and adver-tisers in pursuit of commonly shared societal values. But what is happening now? The invitations from networks and advertisers to social scientists to participate in policy decisions and the formation of self-regulatory guidelines are certainly a step in the right direction. But it is important to note that the dialogue in the United States lags far behind that of other countries. In 1972, Alberta Siegel suggested in her statement at the hearings before a congressional subcommittee that private foundations provide travel fellowships so that producers of American entertain-ment TV could go abroad to learn from those whose television policies and programs were more sensitive to social needs than our own: the English, Dutch, French, Swedish, Canadians (Siegel, 1972). It is, in fact, a sad comment on our lack of societal concern or narrowness of research interests that European social scientists, educators, writers and producers of television have shown far more interest in the whole question of family uses of television.

The Prix Jeunesse Seminars have been devoted to such exchanges and pursuits, and the entire 1975 seminar was on Television and Socialization Processes in the Family (Oeller & Sturm, 1975). While the dialogue among people involved in research and education, practitioners and artists is developing slowly in Europe, it is a continuous effort with impressive results. Not only is the childrens' fare far superior to our own, but the production of programs which are meaningful to families from different social backgrounds are given high priority.

Prospects for Change

At this point, neither the short-term, nor the long-term expectations look very bright. There is no reason to expect widespread changes in government policy nor industry revolution. While the dialogue among social scientists, government, industry and advertisers is promising, we have yet to see any discernible progress. Who would not cheer on such a nascent dialogue, but the concerns of the present symposium remind all of us that in the six years which have elapsed since the Report to the Surgeon-General, American television has changed very little. Further, it seems to me that we have done little to help families understand the meaning of current television fare for children, especially young children. A consistent finding from 1972 until the recent Canadian studies is that mothers of young children use television as a babysitter (Lyle, 1972; Fouts, 1978). The well-known Japanese researcher, Furu, has noted this practice in his own country and has warned that patterns of television viewing are formed in preschool years and that parental influence is most effective at an early age (Furu, 1971). Lyle and Hoffman (1972) as well as Chaffee and McLeod (1972) reported in 1972 that parental attempts to control television with older children were associated with heavy TV viewing. It appears that parental control arises as a response to high television use. But the patterns are already formed. I do not believe that we have made the necessary effort to share our knowledge concerning the importance of early viewing habits with parents of young children or parents-to-be.

Another common practice is that of using television as "background noise" with no one in particular watching it. Although we do not know how widespread the practice is, reference has been made to it for over a decade. Recent Canadian research with school-age children indicates that the more the TV set was on as "background noise", the unhappier the youngster and the more aggressive he or she was in the home (Fouts, 1978). Again, one must wonder if parents understand what "background noise" may mean to a young child.

Education for Watching Television

I would hope to see the development of school curricula devoted to understanding television--its production, function and potential effects. A part of such a curricula would also include critiques of advertising practices and consumer education. Extensions of the curricula would involve adult education and films which could be used by various public service agencies with parents as well as the development of preschool materials. Although the task sounds awesome, it is not as if we should have to start from scratch. Aimee Leifer's research at Harvard with adolescents and young adults in which she investigated the level of understanding of television production and applicability of varieties of content to personal life styles is a fine beginning (Leifer, 1975). In addition, there are some immediate steps which could be taken by teachers and schools to incorporate education for television into existing classes. Audio and visual techniques employed to focus attention and underscore content could be examined in speech or film courses. Media portrayals of males and females and marriage could be evaluated in sex education courses, and so on. There are many possibilities to be explored by creative teachers. I am not suggesting an educational "frill" but an active program to help children and families to cope with television by learning to view programs and advertising critically and defensively.

References

Allouche-Benayoun, B. J. The influence of moving pictures on children and young people. In Oeller, H. and H. Sturm (Eds.), Television and Socialization Processes in the Family. Munich: Verlag Dokumentation, 1975, pp. 137-157.

Ball, S. & Bogatz, G. A. The First Year of Sesame Street: An Evaluation. Princeton, N. J.: Educational Testing Service, 1970.

Berkowitz, L. The contagion of violence: An S-R mediational analysis of some effects of observed aggression. In W. J. Arnold and M. M. Page (Eds.), Nebraska Symposium on Motivation, Vol. 18, Lincoln: University of Nebraska Press, 1970.

Bogatz, G. A. & Ball, S. The Second Year of Sesame Street:
A Continuing Evaluation. Vols. 1 & 2. Princeton:
Educational Testing Service, 1971.

Chaffee, S. H. & McLeod, J. M. Adolescent television use in
the family context. In G. A. Comstock and E. A.
Rubinstein (Eds.), Television and social behavior.
Vol. 3, Television and adolescent aggressiveness.
Washington, D.C.: Government Printing Office, 1972.

Comstock, G. A. & Rubinstein, E. A. (Eds.). Television and
Social Behavior. Vol. 1. Media Content and Control.
Washington: Government Printing Office, 1972(a).

Comstock, G. A. & Rubinstein, E. A. (Eds.). Television and
Social Behavior, Vol. 3. Television and Adolescent
Aggressiveness. Washington: Government Printing
Office, 1972(b).

Comstock, G. A., Rubinstein, E. A. & Murray, J. P. (Eds.).
Television and Social Behavior, Vol. 5. Television's
Effects: Further Explorations. Washington: Govern-
ment Printing Office, 1972.

Fouts, G. Effects of violence on Canadian children. Paper
presented to the International Association of Applied
Psychology, Munich, Germany, August, 1978.

Friedrich, L. K. & Stein, A. H. Aggressive and prosocial
television programs and the natural behavior of preschool children. Monographs of the Society for
Research in Child Development, 1973, 38 (4, Serial
No. 151).

Friedrich, L. K. & Stein, A. H. Prosocial television and
young children: the effects of verbal labeling and
role playing on learning and behavior. Child Development, 1975, 46, 27-38.

Friedrich, L. K., Stein, A. H. & Susman, E. The effects of
prosocial television and environmental conditions on
preschool children. Paper delivered at American
Psychological Association Meetings. 1975 Eric file
document #ED 119815.

Furu, T. The Function of Television for Children and
Adolescents. Tokoyo: Sophia University, 1971.

Gerbner, G., Gross, L., Jackson-Beeck, M., Jeffries-Fox, A.
& Signorielli, N. Violence Profile No. 9. Philadel-
phia: University of Pennsylvania Press, 1978.

Goranson, R. E.   Media violence and aggressive behavior: a review of experimental research.   In L. Berkowitz (Ed.) Advances in experimental psychology.   Vol. 5.   New York: Academic Press, 1970.

Greenberg, B. S., Ericson, P. M., & Vlahos, M.   Children's television behavior as perceived by mother and child. In E. A. Rubinstein, G. A. Comstock, and J. P. Murray (Eds.), Television and social behavior.   Vol. 4.   Television in day-to-day life: patterns of use.   Washington, D. C.:   Government Printing Office, 1972.

Himmelweit, H. T., Oppenheim, A. H. & Vince, P.   Television and the Child.   London: Oxford University Press, 1958.

Huston-Stein, A.   Television and growing up: the medium gets equal time.   Invited address, American Psychological Association Meetings, San Francisco, 1977.

Leifer, A. D.   Research on the socialization influence of television in the United States.   In H. Oeller and H. Sturm (Eds.), Television and Socialization Processes in the Family.   Munich: Verlag Dokumentation, 1975, pp. 26-53.

Leifer, A. D. Children's critical evaluation of television content.   Symposium, American Psychological Association Meetings, Washington, D. C., 1976.

Lesser, G. S.   Children and Television: Lessons from "Sesame Street", New York: Random House, 1974.

Lyle, J.   Television in daily life: patterns of use (Overview).   In E. A. Rubinstein and J. P. Murray (Eds.), Television and social behavior.   Vol. 5.   Television's effects: further explorations.   Washington, D. C.: Government Printing Office, 1972.

Lyle, J. & Hoffman, H.   Children's use of television and other media.   In E. A. Rubinstein, G. A. Comstock and J. P. Murray (Eds.), Television and social behavior. Vol. 4.   Television in day-to-day patterns of use. Washington, D. C.:   Government Printing Office, 1972.

McLeod, J. M., Atkin, C. K. & Chaffee, S. H.   Adolescents, parents and television use: adolescent and other-report measures from the Wisconsin sample.   In G. A. Comstock and E. A. Rubinstein (Eds.), Television and social behavior.   Vol. 3.   Television and adolescent aggressiveness.   Washington, D. C.:   Government Printing Office, 1972.

Murray, J. P., Rubinstein, E. A. & Comstock, G. A. (Eds.).
Television and social behavior. Vol. 2. Television
and social learning. Washington, D. C.: Government
Printing Office, 1972.

Oeller, H. & Sturm, H. (Eds.). Television and Socialization
Processes in the Family. Munich: Verlag Dokumentation,
1975.

Parke, R. E., Berkowitz, L., Leyens, J. P., West, S. &
Sebastian, R. J. Film violence and aggression: a
field experimental analysis. Journal of Social
Issues, 1974.

Robinson, J. P. & Bachman, J. G. Television viewing habits
and aggression. In G. A. Comstock and E. A. Rubinstein (Eds.), Television and social behavior. Vol. 3.
Television and adolescent aggressiveness. Washington,
D. C.: Government Printing Office, 1972.

Rubinstein, E. A., Comstock, G. A. & Murray, J. P. (Eds.),
Television and social behavior. Vol. 4. Television
in day-to-day life: patterns of use. Washington,
D. C.: Government Printing Office, 1972.

Rubinstein, E. A. Television and the young viewer. American Scientist, 1978, 66, 685-693.

Salomon, G. Effects of encouraging Israeli mothers to co-
observe"Sesame Street" with their five-year-olds.
Unpublished manuscript. The Hebrew University of
Jerusalem, 1973.

Schramm, W., Lyle, J. & Parker, E. B. Television in the
lives of our children. Stanford, California: Stanford
University Press, 1961.

Siegel, A. "Statement" at the Hearings before the Sub-
committee on Communications of the Committee on
Commerce of the United States Senate. Ninety-Second
Congress. March 21, 1972. U. S. Government Printing
Office, Serial Number 92-52, pp. 62-64.

Stein, A. H. & Friedrich, L. K. The impact of television
on children and youth. In E. M. Hetherington, J. W.
Hagen, R. Kron and A. H. Stein (Eds.), Review of Child
Development Research. Vol. 5. Chicago: University
of Chicago Press, 1975, pp. 183-256.

Steinfeld, J. A. TV violence is harmful. In: Reader's
Digest, April, 1973, pp. 37-45.

Steuer, F. B., Applefield, J. M. & Smith, R. Televised
    aggression and the interpersonal aggression of pre-
    school children. Journal of Experimental Child
    Psychology, 1971, 11, 442-447.

Surgeon-General's Scientific Advisory Committee on Tele-
    vision and Social Behavior. Television and growing
    up: The impact of televised violence. Washington:
    Government Printing Office, 1972.

Wells, W. D. Television and aggression: replication of an
    experimental field study. Unpublished manuscript,
    University of Chicago Graduate School of Business,
    1973.

3. Ethnopsychiatric Dimensions in Family Violence

Research on violence in the family is currently in a
state of ferment. Two recently published collections of
papers, Violence and the Family,edited by J.P. Martin (Martin,
1978) and Family Violence, edited by John Eekelaar and Sanford
Katz, (Eekelar and Katz, 1978), illustrate at a glance that
the subject matter is being approached from a variety of per-
spectives, through a number of different disciplines, and
that there is some disagreement, even mild controversy among
those now active in this field. There also seem to be a few,
general points of agreement. It is apparently agreed that
1) we are dealing with a wide spectrum of physical aggression,
from mild to severe; 2) that the cut-off points for the tar-
get behaviors labelled "the battered child" and "the battered
wife" syndromes vary considerably, in accordance with differing criteria from study to study; 3) that both "battering"
and lesser forms of violence, such as "hitting" have been
and still are under-reported and are therefore more ubiquitous
than has been generally realized; 4) that only an as yet
undetermined minor portion of this violence is associated
with substantial, intrapsychic pathology (i.e. the "clinical"
portion); 5) that political and "social movement" forces,
such as "feminism" and "child advocacy" are responsible for
the recent interest in the phenomenon and have perhaps induced some exaggerated fears in public awareness, as well as
some bias among investigators; and 6) that violence in the
family is generated by a variety of factors--in other words,
there is no simple cause, either situational, psychological,
economic, legal, or socio-cultural. All these sources of the
behavior interact with each other in what Murray Straus has
called "the combined effect" (Straus, 1979).

My presentation today will focus on just one of these
interacting factors: the contrasting sub-cultural rules,
norms and issues which provide the occasions for the expression of violence in ethnic families. Since there are many

different ethnic groups in the United States, it would be an
impossible task to cover the subject of ethnicity and violence in an exhaustive fashion. Nor is a comprehensive survey important to the goal of this paper. Rather, I want to
demonstrate that even in selecting out for discussion just
one of the many factors involved in the expression of violence, the complications become manifold. Nevertheless,
despite the difficulties and the necessary qualifications
and cautions which any discussion of ethnicity entails, the
approach is an important one. Too often the family is discussed as if it were a universal, monolithic, unvarying and
easily understood (because we all live in families) showpiece
entitled, THE AMERICAN FAMILY.

Qualifications for Comparisons

Let us begin with some qualifications. I intend to
contrast Italian-American, Irish-American and mainstream,
Waspish, middle-class American families with respect to some
of the issues which give rise to violence. I also want to
briefly discuss some contrasts in child-rearing practices
concerned with the control of aggressions. Finally, I want
to contrast all three of these European-derived families with
the Tahitian family style, because this particular variant of
Oceanic Polynesian culture is so famed for the gentleness,
friendliness, and humility of its adult products.

Such a comparison entails a number of risks. The description of the basic cultural values brought by Italian and
Irish families from their country of origin to the United
States is based on studies carried out in those countries
earlier in the 20th Century. To be sure, the descriptions
are reasonably valid for the time when many, but not all,
first generation immigrants came to this country. In the
meantime, however, both Ireland and Italy have undergone
socio-cultural change in directions which have been insuf-
ficiently investigated. More important, in the process of
acculturation and hyphenation, Irish and Italian families
have taken on some American main-stream values and have lost
some of their original cultural life-styles. At the same
time, the main-stream, middle-class, Anglo-Saxon derived
family styles have been themselves undergoing change. In
the context of all this variation and social change, it is
difficult to make any generalizations that can withstand
challenge, or that can avoid the risk of unrealistic stereo-
typing. Let the audience (the reader) therefore, take what I
have to say with several grains of salt.

Despite a well-deserved skepticism, there are two reasons
for pursuing the kind of comparison proposed in this paper.

The first is the remarkable persistence of some of the basic contrasts across generations revealed in our own studies of Italian-Americans and Irish-Americans (Papajohn and Spiegel, 1975); a finding that has been confirmed through a wholly different method by Greeley and McCready (1975). An article on Italian-Americans by Elizabeth Stone which recently appeared in The New York Times Sunday Magazine (1978) provides some touching anecdotal references to the stability of Italian values. So, in spite of its somewhat shaky empirical foundations, the staying-power of a cultural inheritance cannot be lightly dismissed.

The second, and more important, reason is concerned with a conceptual issue. When one highlights--to be sure, at the risk of exaggeration--the contrasting occasions for family violence between cultural or sub-cultural groups, one gets the impression that violence has to be re-invented, or at least, redesigned, for each group during the history of its evolution as a distinct culture. Of course, it may be derived from the universal propensity for aggression which is considered by some to be characteristic of our species. But the social and situational materials assembled into the final product are so different as to resemble the different tissues that are assembled into superficially similar structures in the course of biological evolution--like the wings of the butterfly compared to the wings of the bird, or the fish-like lure of the freshwater clam, Lampsilis, compared to the fish-like lure of the angler fish, ascribed by Stephen Jay Gould (1979) to a "parts available" principle. If family violence arises out of "parts available," then national policy, whether preventive or remedial, has to be based upon an understanding of how those parts function in different ethnic groups. This policy issue is similar to the emphasis given by Murray Straus (1979) to the need to understand "normal violence"--that is, to understand the cultural norms used to justify violence.

Italian-American Families

For example, among the Italian-Americans there is a rather high tolerance for the expression of aggressive behavior, between husband and wife, parents and children, and among the children themselves. This is part of the expressive behavior of Italian life styles. Suddenly expressed hitting, cuffing or verbal abuse can be just as suddenly followed by loving, kissing and embracing movements. Both behaviors involve the physical closeness which is important to Italian family interactions. But, the context for the aggression tends to involve situations which cast shame or embarrassment upon the individual or the family. The public reputation of the family and the honor of the family lineage must be main-

tained at all costs. In the economically hard-pressed Southern Italian countryside from which most Italian-Americans
emigrated there were always gossips and tongue-waggers ready
to besmirch the family honor, and suspiciousness between
rival groups ran high. Thus, making a visibly appropriate
aggressive display in an often dramatically tinged public
appearance avoided public embarrassment and had the highest
priority.

A scene from the film, Saturday Night Fever, succinctly
illustrates some of these issues. The story centers around
an Italian-American family living in Brooklyn and this scene
occurs at the dinner table. The son Tony, who is the hero
of the film, played by John Travolta, has been preparing to
go to the disco dance. He has spent a lot of time selecting
his clothes and shampooing and arranging his hair and he is
now sitting at the dinner table covered in a sheet to protect
against spotting. A fight breaks out after the sister makes
a wisecrack about Tony. The children begin hitting each
other. Then the parents begin hitting the children. The
cuffing goes around the table several times until the father
hits Tony in the head. Up to this point, no one has been
particularly surprised or upset. The aggression appears to
be normal, everyday activity. But now Tony sits back and
with a look of shocked surprise and indignation on his face,
says to his father, "You hit me in the hair!" Having his
hairdo damaged just before the disco is, apparently, out of
bounds. The family is so taken aback at this development
that as if by total consensus, the aggressions stop as suddenly as they started. After all, it is important that Tony
should enhance the family's reputation by making a good
appearance at the disco.

Later, when Tony wins the first prize at the disco
competition, the issue of reputation and group honor comes
into even sharper focus. Tony has been moving away from the
collaterally organized, Italian values toward American individualism. Because he thinks he did not merit it, he refuses
to keep his first prize and turns it over to the second choice
Puerto Rican dancers who, in his opinion, were superior.
Feeling rivalrous with the Puerto Ricans, his Italian-American
friends are, at first, unbelieving, then infuriated. It is
as if Tony had dishonored the whole community. Somewhat un-
focussed but intense sexual and physical violence immediately
follows this event.

One aspect of what Peter Loizos (1978) has called "the
honor code" of rural Southern Italian families features the
unquestioned dominance and superiority of the male, the
presumed moral inferiority and sexual weakness of the female,

and the responsibility of fathers and brothers to protect
the virginity of unmarried daughters. Along with this responsibility goes the right to punish an unmarried daughter--
often brutally--for any breath of suspicion of sexual contact
with a boy. Marriages are usually arranged, based not on
love but on economic considerations. Suspicion of premarital
sex in the easily seduced daughter not only puts a blot on
the family's reputation but also makes any marriage much more
costly to arrange in terms of doweries. This context for the
precipitation of violence persists in many Italian-American
families. In the film Saturday Night Fever the stigma
attached to an unmarried girl who "puts out" and the anger
aroused by an unmarried girl who emits ambiguous cues through
responding too readily are among the principle occasions for
an outbreak of violence.

Irish-American Families

With Irish-Americans the occasions for violence are concerned more with an inner sense of sin than with external
worry about shame, honor and reputation. As with Italians,
the content of the precipitating incident in the family often
centers around the possible sexual transgression of an unmarried daughter, but the emphasis is moralistic and the
punishment is designed to instill guilt rather than shame.

The cultural origins of this behavior spring from two
sources. In Ireland the Catholic Church has traditionally
been harsh about matters of sin and temptation while the
Italian versions of Catholicism has been softer and more joy-
ful. A sign of this distinction is the Irish emphasis on
fasting compared to the Italian emphasis on feasting--the
fiesta--for religious holidays. Secondly, with regard to
sexual behavior rural Southern Ireland traditionally had the
oldest age of marriage of any Western European country. Young
men were unable to marry until they had inherited some land
to farm and the farms had been cut up so often that there was
little land available for distribution across generations.
Additionally, the father was unwilling to turn over land to ·
his young sons because then he would have nothing to do. Em-
igration was a solution used by some but not enough of the
many children in Irish families. Though the daughters were
expected to remain virgins until marriage, the sons, whose
sexual behavior was not so rigidly controlled, looked for
sexual partners. Thus, the possibility of sin was always
around the corner, and parents were understandably anxious
about their daughters.

In the Irish-American families included in our own
studies the training to be aware of and to resist sin and

temptation began in early childhood. Parents tended to use a technique which we called "confession extraction." For example, if a mother returned home to find the sugar spilled or a cookie jar broken, she would turn to the first child to cross her path with the angry question,"Why did you do that?" Faced with such an accusation, the children soon learned to adopt two kinds of responses. The first was an angry and indignant denial, such as "What are you talking about? I didn't do it. He (or she) did it!" while pointing to another sibling. The accusation would then be repeated to the next child and the next child punctuated by the stock denials, until one child confessed: "I did it. I didn't mean to. I'll never do it again!" with appropriate tears. The promise not to do it again was not too meaningful. What was important was that either a vigorous denial or a contrite confession served to ease the mother's anxiety. What she was trying to teach the children was the awareness of sin--of giving way to a temptation for engaging in forbidden behavior. The vigorous denial was a sign that the accusation was taken seriously, that the concept of sin was being internalized. The confession had the same meaning. Simultaneously, the parent was teaching a particularly moralistic view of human nature: that the power of the will is weak; that temptations, especially of the flesh, are strong; and that one must be ever on guard against sin.

When violence breaks out in Irish-American families it is usually in the context of accusations and denials. Of course, such exchanges can occur in the course of any quarrel, among any group of people. If guilt is strongly internalized, then it tends to be projected, making the accusations and denials part of the same, fundamental process. Thus, in the Irish case, the initial content of the quarrel tends to fade out, to become relatively featureless, while the accusations and denials take over as the priority issue. In fact, process becomes more important than substance, making it difficult to get back to the basics of the violence so that the conflict can be resolved. The quarrel, and its associated violence in fact, develops an autonomous life of its own. It becomes protracted and feud-like. This seems to be a characteristic of the prolonged "troubles" between Catholics and Protestants currently disrupting life in Northern Ireland.

Mainstream American Families

In mainstream American families neither shame over family dishonor nor guilt over family sinning form the occasions for violence. Guilt and shame can both be present but in a different context. These families are guided by the norms of individualism and personal achievement. Hus-

bands respond aggressively to a wife's reproaches, overt or
implied, of failure, in either sexual prowess or occupational
success. Husbands counterattack with complaints of the wife's
incompetence in domestic house-care, as a mother, or in bed.
Both parents blame each other as the childrens' growing
search for autonomy and individualism turns them away from
the mother and father, sometimes in a rebellious fashion.
Or the children feel neglected and angry because of the time
the parents spend out of the home in search of a career.
The children develop competitive envy over who is doing better in school or who has more friends.

It is the sense of inferiority and the frustration of
dependency needs that gives rise to violence in families
oriented to achievement values. The child-battering mother
was herself alternately neglected or abused in childhood,
and she feels a failure in motherhood when her child cries
too much. She has little mothering to give her child. As
Murray Straus has already pointed out (1979) the isolated,
urban, nuclear family lacks the network of an extended family
or relatives to give assistance when the parents are hard-
pressed. The neglected or abused child has no refuge in the
family of a close relation, nowhere to go until old enough to
run away. And there are no caring persons around to stop the
violence once it breaks out.

Cross-Cultural Gains and Losses

There is a high price to be paid for every cultural plan
of family living. The price of the Italian "honor code" is
high in violence but it provides enormous security for those
who adhere to it. The Irish concern with sin is costly in
violence and in other respects but it is complemented by
great courage and high humor in the face of adversity. The
American family's craving for individual achievement breeds
loneliness and worry about one's "personality" and about
success in social relations, as well as broken marriages and
violence; but it is responsible for the enormous achievements
of our technological society.

Tahitian Family Life

The Tahitians of the South Pacific, as I said at the
outset, are known for their gentle ways and peaceful family
life. How does that work and what are its costs?

According to Robert Levy (1973), from whose writing this
description is borrowed, Tahitians live close together in
small, communally organized villages. There is very little
privacy in the open thatched dwellings and village pathways.

The family living is based on a traditional subsistence economy--fishing and small farming--which has changed little over hundreds of years. Under these circumstances, both aggression and personal ambition are rigidly controlled because such behaviors would be too disruptive of group life. Humility and pleasant, friendly behavior are highly valued, as is conformity to the traditional ways. Aggression and violence are inhibited partly by shame and embarrassment but, in a more important manner, by easily verbalized fear-- fear of causing trouble and fear of getting into trouble by exhibiting disapproved behavior. Although courageous under physical stress, the Tahitians are proud of their caution and timidity in social relationships, because these attributes keep village life untroubled. Aggression and violence may break out among men during drinking bouts on holiday occasions, and, rarely, in the course of domestic quarrels. Such events merely highlight the general smoothness and integrations of social life.

Childrearing practices in Tahiti are aimed at inducing docility, mainly through fear-producing techniques. After infancy, small children are watched by somewhat older child- ren who in turn are the responsibility of their older sib- lings, while the mother or father or another relative monitors the scene from a distance. Parents are not indulgent of the children after infancy and good behavior is seldom rewarded. The assumption is that the child will learn of his own accord, mainly by imitation of others. What is important is that the child learn to fear misbehavior. Children are angrily scold- ed or threatened with being hit but such threats are seldom carried out. The principle fear-inducing technique involves the use of accidental injuries. If a child falls down and hurts himself, the injury will be ascribed to some previous act of misbehavior with the statement, "You deserved it." Sympathy for the injured child or comforting are not forth- coming. Thus the fear of misbehavior is generalized and made impersonal, and it is consistently reinforced. Since the children in these villages display intense physical activity, they are apt to hurt themselves frequently.

Despite the somewhat distant and impersonal attitude of the parents, children almost always feel wanted. In part this is due to the practice of voluntary adoption. Pre- marital intercourse is socially acceptable and the young unmarried mothers often do not wish to keep the first or second child born of such unions. There is always a parent or some close relative eager to have a baby in the home. Older parents whose children have left the home are especially on the lookout for a child to adopt. In fact, a struggle can ensue between a young mother who wishes to keep her baby and an older relative who wants to adopt it. Thus, whether children are kept by their biological parents or are adopted, they live in the knowledge of having been wanted. In the rare instances of neglect or discord, the child can always leave home and be accepted by a relative. Thus, the integration of the child into the home and into the tightly-knit, wider community proceeds smoothly along well-trodden, traditional paths.

What are the costs of this interpersonal harmony? In the eyes of Westerners the suppression of individualism and personal initiative seems too high a price to pay for the uniform charm and friendliness and the physical beauty of the Tahitians and their islands. But that is a value judgment lacking any objective qualities. Westerners are also disappointed with the lack of preparation for and acceptance of change, the sameness and simpleness of life styles year after year and decade after decade. This is also a value judgment derived from a future-oriented culture constantly preparing for complexity and rapid social change. But it has some objective attributes. The future is coming to the Society Islanders.

Ethnic Values and Technological Change

Technological changes are making their inexorable voyages around the globe. Tahitians are increasingly deserting the villages for the cash economy of Papeete, the capital city, and tourism is flourishing in the outer islands. The Club Meds and the Bali-Bali resorts bring paying customers from all over the world for a week or two in a tropical paradise. The beaches of Bora-Bora, Huahine and Moorea are carpeted with white bodies glistening with suntan lotion in the effort to acquire the copper-colored skin of the Polynesians. When families move out of the traditional social controls of the villages, the carefully dovetailed internal and external inhibitions of aggression tend to dissolve. Embarrassment and shame exert their powers mainly among people who know each other well. The fear of the stranger and of getting into trouble lose their effect when there are so many strangers around and when trouble becomes increasingly common. The acceptance of new ways among the young of Western music, dance and clothing mediated by films and television, loosens the traditional authority of the older generation. As a result, use of alcohol and drugs and outbreaks of aggression and violence in younger people are increasing social problems. The cash economies cannot supply enough jobs nor replace the social security of the traditional villages. The paradise lost did not prepare its people for the complexeties of the technology gained.

Violence and Child-Rearing Practices

In conclusion, I want to stress again that I have max-
imized the differences in the contexts of family violence
for the sake of comparing ethnic variables. The analysis
which I have offered is superficial and overgeneralized.
A richer, more detailed inquiry would illustrate the widespread overlap of factors from group to group. But, a more
detailed examination would also strengthen the main point
I wish to make: that there is a special--a modal--way in
which each cultural or national group fashions its child-
rearing practices for the control or loss of control of the
type of violence which is apt to break out among its families, and within its wider, societal networks.

Sensitivity to this issue is important because of a
general psychological process which Martin Symonds (1978)
has labelled "identification with the victim in the aggressor." We all understand, perhaps only dimly, that the aggressor attacks his victim because he feels himself to be
victimized in some way. This principle becomes important
in psychotherapy as the therapist finds out precisely how
the aggressor feels victimized, owing to what childhood
event or current circumstance. But it is also important
for the general education of the public. As the widespread
presence of violence comes increasingly to public awareness,
people react with shock or horror. Understanding eludes
them, and they feel helpless and frightened. If there were
a better public knowledge of the precise ways in which violence is generated or its controls broken down in the families of different ethnic and social groups, then at least
the horror--the unbelievable quality--of violence would be
diminished. Such knowledge could lead to improved methods
of control among law enforcement personnel. It might even
give rise to some effective methods of prevention. And
that would be a blessing for us all.

References

Eekelaar, John M. and Katz, Sanford N. editors,; Family Violence; An International and Interdisciplinary Study. Butterworths, Toronto, 1978.

Gould, Stephen Jay. "This View of Life" Natural History, January, 1979.

Goealey, Andrew M. and McCready, William C. "The Transmission of Cultural Heritage; The Case of the Irish and the Italians," in Ethnicity; Theory and Experiences Nathan Glazer and Daniel P. Moynahan editors, Harvard University Press, Cambridge, Mass., 1975.

Levy, Robert I. The Tahitians; Mind and Experience in the Society Islands. University of Chicago Press, Chicago, Illinois, 1973.

Loizos, Peter. "Violence and the Family; Some Mediterranean Examples." Violence and the Family. J.P. Martin editor. Wiley, N.Y.C., 1978.

Papajohn, John and Spiegel, John P. Transactions in Families, A Modern Approach for Resolving Cultural and Generational Conflict. Jossey-Bass, San Fransisco, 1975.

Stone, Elizabeth. "Its Still Hard to Grow Up Italian" New York Times Magazine, December 17, 1978.

Straus, Murray A. "A Sociological Perspective on the Causes of Family Violence," pp. 7-31, this volume.

Symonds, Martin. Personal Communication.

Discussion:
Violence and the Family
in Perspective

My interest in violence as a scientific issue began
more than a quarter century ago. In the summer of 1952, I
found myself participating in an official act of violence.
This was an execution--a hanging--at the Iowa State Peniten-
tiary in Fort Madison. Two medical examiners were required
by law to be present in order to certify to the fact and time
of death. The regular prison physician was an old friend;
his regular medical helper was away; I was passing through
town and found myself serving as a last minute substitute to
do my friend a favor.

The impact of that experience was considerable, and led
me to inspect a number of related issues. For example, I
came to realize that if my friend and I, as physicians, had
not participated in the execution, under the law it could
not have taken place at that time. The State would then have
faced three alternatives: to find physicians who were willing to serve; to change the law; or to forego the execution
indefinitely.

Beyond such interesting technicalities, however, the
larger implications of that legalized homicide caused me to
turn my attention to the question of whether such violence
was in fact necessary to reduce greater violence. The
many intervening years of pursuing this and related questions
in depth have exposed me to a great deal of information
about the death penalty, much of which is unknown to the general public, some of which is even paradoxical. Briefly, the
weight of evidence clearly suggests that in the United States,
at least, executions have stimulated more violence than they
have prevented. The death penalty emerges as a grisly lottery
which generally impedes rather than enhances the administration of criminal justice.

Table 1. Violent Crime in the United States, 1960-1975:
Rate per 100,000 Population

Year	Total Violent Crimes	Types of Violent Crimes			
		Homicide*	Forcible Rape	Armed Robbery	Aggravated Assault
1960	159.6	5.0	9.5	59.9	85.2
1965	198.3	5.1	12.0	71.3	109.9
1970	361.0	7.8	18.6	171.5	163.1
1975	481.5	9.6	26.3	218.2	227.4

* Murder and non-negligent manslaughter.
Source: FBI Unified Crime Report, published annually.

The recent upsurge of desire by the American people to
utilize the death penalty again without a doubt derives
partly from our national tradition of violence. However,
it is also unquestionably in part a reaction by the American
public to the recent epidemic of violence which has plagued
the United States (Table 1).

In light of our awareness of this epidemic, the rise
of violence involving families, including child abuse and
wife beating, can be seen as part of a larger whole. To
comprehend the totality is a massive assignment. Several
national commissions and an increasing number of well organized research programs still leave us short of such a com-
prehension. Nevertheless, I am willing to offer my personal
glimpse of an overview so that the several excellent studies
described in this symposium will be perceived in the context of that overview. Perhaps I should begin by expressing
my great respect for those whose studies on violence have
been presented here, and my appreciation for the difficulties inevitably encountered in such work.

The UCLA Violence Center

Together with a large group of colleagues at the
University of California, Los Angeles, I recently undertook
to organize a comprehensive center for research on violence.
This soon became known as the "Violence Center" (although
its official designation was the Center for the Study of
Life Threatening Behavior) and was surrounded by storms of
controversy during 1974. Attacks upon the Center were

primarily in terms of the putative dangers it would post.
Allegations were made that research on violence inevitably
would lead to the abuse of human subjects, to experimenta-
tion upon prisoners, to the implantation of electrodes in
heads of unsuspecting minority group members, to unwonted
psychosurgery, and to the malapplication of any new knowledge by an implacable government which would undoubtedly
use information on how to control violence to control all
forms of political and social dissidence.

The UCLA Center for the Study of Life Threatening
Behavior had published a clear protocol indicating its intention to study (with utmost ethical regard for human subjects) topics such as suicide, homicide, rape, child abuse,
the influence of alcohol and drugs on behavior, animal studies, etc. However, as part of a highly emotional but well-
organized local and national campaign to destroy the Center--
a campaign based on outright lies--the UCLA program was
portrayed as an example of grave scientific and professional
impropriety. The abuses popularized in such works of fiction
as "A Clockwork Orange," "One Flew Over the Cuckoo's Nest,"
and "Terminal Man" were involved. In the end a joint federal
and state commitment of some 4.5 million dollars to support
the first three years of this research was blocked by the
California Legislature, pending their further review and
assignment of permission to proceed. The review never took
place; the permission was never received; the funds were
diverted to other agencies (e.g., police departments) and
the organized violence research program at UCLA died aborning.

In reviewing this extraordinary experience, which is
described in detail elsewhere (Litman and West, 1975), I
have noted a number of lessons to be learned. It is not
my intention to review them all here. One issue, however,
that was raised repeatedly, even by apparently sincere critics, was that it would be wrong for UCLA to study interpersonal or individual violence, or violence limited to
small groups such as the family, when the most important
issues lay in the larger sphere of collective violence and its
social causes. It was repeatedly charged that to study the
violent individual and/or his victim was to shift public attention and resources away from the larger social roots of
violence. As the critics seemed already to know with great
certainty what these were, any research would have been unnecessary; all that was needed was a vast program of social
reform or, in the view of many of the antagonists, political
revolution. The consensus of the amalgamated opposition to
the UCLA Center was that to study violence using the models
of biomedical or behavioral science would be to do the public
a disservice.

Collective Versus Interpersonal Violence

Unquestionably collective violence is mankind's most important problem. So far in the twentieth century, perhaps 120 million people have died violently on this planet, mostly as a consequence of collective violence: wars, revolutions, persecutions, pogroms, tribal conflicts, and other acute and chronic intergroup strife of all kinds. However, research on this problem has been going on for some time. The opponents of research on interpersonal violence assume that collective violence and interpersonal violence are the same. In this they are profoundly mistaken.

In my view it is essential to differentiate collective violence from the individual and family violence which is the object of our concern here, and which accounts for most of the epidemic of violence in the United States in the last 15 years. This differentiation can be made in various ways. However, from the point of view of behavioral science, perhaps the most interesting is the difference of motivation between most of those persons involved in collective violence and those involved in interpersonal violence. There is a great likelihood that emotional or mental disturbance or disorder will <u>not</u> be a major motivational force in the former group, and that it will be in the latter.

The biosocial imperatives that so frequently in human history have led groups of people into conflict with other groups has been the subject of considerable commentary by philosophers, religionists, historians, politicians, and more recently, behavioral scientists, whose expertise range from psychoanalysis to ethology. My own formulation of this problem has been reported elsewhere (West 1967), and I shall not review it here. Let me only comment that I do not assign to instinct (the so-called "territorial imperative") a significant role in the phenomenology of collective violence among humans.

For our purposes here it should suffice to point out that the model of collective violence is war, and that in modern warfare and modern armies, only the healthiest and socially best adjusted members of the population are chosen to take part in this particular mass destruction of man toward man. A modern army, navy or air force is unlikely to accept for service a volunteer who has a history of criminal violence. Instead, positive qualities are sought in recruiting good soldiers, sailors, and airmen--qualities quite different from those found in most of the persons responsible for the sharp rise in statistics on violence in the United States. The best recruit to the armed forces

should be physically and mentally healthy, intelligent,
well-educated, emotionally stable, outgoing, have been a
member of appropriate social groups (e.g., church, scouts,
unions, fraternal organizations, business clubs, etc.), and
willing to engage in harmonious mutual relationships with
others of his own kind (i.e., comrades) with whom he can
identify, toward whom he feels loyalty, and for whom he is
willing to risk his life.

The body count of victims of violence in this country
is composed mostly of family members, friends, drinking com-
panions, relatives, neighbors, or neighborhood dwellers of
individuals who have acted out their violent impulses.
Here we see violence directed not toward some distant group
of strangers conveniently identified as "the enemy" and
assigned attributes antithetical to our own, but rather
toward the perpetrator's real family or that larger pseudo-
family called the community, made of individuals very much
like himself. In other words, collective violence is at
least seemingly motivated by a desire to <u>protect</u> the "family"
from those who are seen to threaten it and who are different
from it, while interpersonal violence is largely directed
<u>toward</u> other members of the family or of the community.

From the foregoing it must be clear that I do not regard research on violence as a unified field of study. I
believe that grievous error has crept into the theoretical
formulations of those who tend to look upon violence as a
unitary phenomenon throughout the species. Such studies
do not differentiate among clashes between one animal or one
person and another, and collective or organized assaults by
whole groups on other groups. In my view it is here that the
theoretical speculations of Robert Ardrey and similar thinkers
break down; and it is here that studies of family violence
provide important insights into the peculiarly human basis
for violence among humans. Such insights reveal that anal-
ogies from studies of other animals possess extremely limited values in looking at violence in the human family setting.

The Spectrum of Interpersonal Violence

It should also be emphasized that violence in the family
context must itself be studied, not as a unitary phenomenon
but in the context of a spectrum of behaviors from generally
accepted to generally abhorred. The socially sanctioned
physical hurting behavior in the home is often related to
the alleged inculcation of values such as discipline, respect,
development of conscience, and appreciation of the difference
between right and wrong, etc.

Occasional slapping or spanking (while it is, in my view, both unnecessary and undesirable) is so widely accepted as appropriate behavior within the family context that it probably cannot be very closely compared to the behavior of the parent who batters his or her baby to death. The person who in the height of sexual passion gently bites or slightly scratches a lover might be described as incorporating violence into the erotic component of life, but such behavior can be differentiated both qualitatively and quantitatively from that of a man who has buried under his house 32 bodies of homosexual rape victims. Somewhere along the continuum between such extremes it becomes reasonable to make a qualitative judgment between behavior that is not necessarily unhealthy and behavior that is clearly very sick.

Those of us in the health-related professions find that most of the violence and its aftermath that washes up on our stretch of the beach is of the "sick" variety. We see it in the emergency rooms, the wards, the clinics, the courts. In fact, it is remarkable that we had not studied it more than we have. In this respect the present symposium marks a worthy step in the right direction. Furthermore, while the UCLA Center limited its functional definition of "violence" to mean "life-threatening behavior" (including all non-collective human behavior that deliberately takes life or threatens to do so even though it falls short), the spectral analysis of hurtful behavior in the family was also seen as a valid and highly relevant approach, even though we excluded those behaviors deemed less than life-threatening from our immediate area of focus.

Self-Directed and Other-Directed Violence

Insufficient attention has been directed to the non-specific aspect of certain destructive emotions and impulses in man, which inevitably leads to an inspection of the relationship between homicide and suicide. It was on this account that suicide was included in the array of topics that UCLA classified as "violent." There are a number of reasons to link homicide and suicide together, not only because of their direct correlations, but also because of some intervening variables which correlate with both.

It has been the experience of those who operate the suicide prevention center in Los Angeles that somewhere between 10 and 20 percent of the calls they receive appear to be homicide prevention calls. A certain number of people fear that they may commit an act of violence but aren't sure whether the life-threatening behavior will be directed toward

themselves, toward others, or both. Noting from my own
clinical experience the high frequency of histories of suicidal attempts in people who subsequently attempted or committed homicide, I found myself greatly intrigued by the important study by D. J. West (from the Cambridge University
Institute of Criminology), tracing the subsequent behavior
of people who committed homicide in England. West found that,
over a period of many years, more than half of all English
murderers had subsequently attempted suicide, and that one-
third ended up killing themselves (West, D.J., 1966). A
similar study by Siciliano in Denmark of 545 homicides
over 28 years revealed that more than 42 percent of the
killers subsequently killed themselves (Siciliano, 1961).
In the United States where the murder rate is much higher,
the immediate links to suicide are much less frequent.
Nevertheless, connections between suicidal and homicidal
impulses are far more powerful than we used to believe, and
they work in both directions. Karl Menninger once said
that every suicide is half a number. Now we know that many
murderers, and other violent individuals, are often likely
to be powerfully self-destructive people. Incidentally, this
provides an additional insight into the paradoxical effect
of the death penalty. My own studies indicate that a certain
number of murderers commit homicide primarily to obtain executions for themselves. In other words, they attempt to
commit suicide by committing murder (West, 1975).

Alcohol and Violence

     It seems clear from available data that both in the
United States and in other Western countries alcohol is
involved in nearly half of all violent deaths. These
deaths include homicides, suicides, and fatal accidents in
adults. Of the last, probably more are deliberately or
subintentionally suicidal than we realize. The association
between alcohol abuse and both fatal and nonfatal acts of
violence is very high and very well known. In Europe there
is a general association between the incidence of violence
and the incidence of alcoholism in most of the countries for
which comparable data are available. These national differences tend to persist, at least for several generations,
in ethnic groups transplanted to the United States, Canada
or Australia, and are much more reliable epidemiological
prognosticators than, say, religion or certain other factors
that transcend national boundaries.

     It is important to keep in mind that although alcoholism
and violence tend to correlate among Europeans, the connection between alcohol abuse and violent behavior is also

apparently culture-bound. While it may be argued that alcohol
has disinhibitory effects on behavior ("unleashing the passions," as it were), anthropological studies clearly reveal
that cultural factors are involved. Thus, while some Indian
tribes use alcohol to release or to justify violent behavior,
others do not become violent no matter how drunk they get,
leading investigators to conclude that the weight of cross-
cultural research demonstrates that alcohol has no biological
property which necessarily causes violence (MacAndrew and
Edgerton, 1969).

Cultural Factors

In this symposium we have heard John Spiegel's fascinating description of the way Tahitians have been changing
as they are becoming Westernized. His account reminded me
of my own inquiry into the Tahitian culture--in search
of paradise. Some years ago I was looking for cross-cultural markers of the inclination toward collective violence.
The few remaining relatively isolated cultures, about which
we have good historical or direct observational data, might
be considered experiments of nature. (In fact, I believe
these relatively pure, relatively special cultures to be
the world's most rapidly disappearing scientific natural
resource; their study during the remainder of the twentieth
century should receive the highest possible priority.)

Captain Cook described Tahiti as a paradise of golden-
skinned, beautiful people who greeted him and his sailors
with open arms. Apparently they had no fear of strangers.
In fact, they gave them food, drink, shelter and affection
without restraint. The legend of the Tahitian paradise, and
of the Tahitian as a non-violent person, has really come down
to us practically unchanged since Captain Cook's day. However, when you go into Tahitian history a little further, it
turns out that everything wasn't as peaceful in paradise
as it seemed. In fact, there was a war going on between
the Tahitians at the harbor end of the island (where Captain Cook landed) and the Tahitians at the other end of
the island. These two groups (racially identical) regarded
each other as mortal enemies at that time. An important
part of the reason that the first group of Tahitians em-
braced Captain Cook (and his magical ship with the great
sails, minions with muskets, and the rest) was to enlist
them and their mysterious powers as allies in the war against
the traditional enemies at the other end of the island (Moorehead, 1966). There was a fair amount of warfare in various
parts of Polynesia later on because he failed to realize
that even in paradise appearances could be deceiving.

Nevertheless, it is important to note that the
Polynesians, who are very kindly toward their children, experienced very little violence in the family setting--at
least until the modern day when the depredations of civilization began to have their impact. They were enthusiastic
about collective violence (note the history of the Maori in
New Zealand before the white man's advent), but the interpersonal violence was rare among them.

This brings me, finally, to West's Law: one that has derived from my recent return to a concentration upon individual psychodynamic and intra-familial factors in shaping the
violent behaviors of individuals, especially violent behaviors
of the "sickest" kind. West's Law holds that violence out
equals violence in squared, through time. $(V_O)=(V_I)^2$ This
is meant to state that even a little bit of violence experienced or taken in by a child can result in a great deal
of violence perpetrated or acted out by that child as an
adolescent or adult later on. It isn't only the battering
parent who turns out to have been a battered, harshly treated
or cruelly neglected child. A great many of the most violent
persons in our society, when they are studied individually,
prove to have come out of terribly disturbed family situations, in which they were subjected to extraordinary cruelty
of various kinds when they were quite young.

I could give you a number of examples. One might suffice. A young psychiatrist who learned from an interested
colleague of our increasing preoccupation with this phenomenon returned to his duty station at Leavenworth (the Army's
prison or "disciplinary barracks"), where some of the patho-
logically violent soldiers are confined. At that time there
were at Leavenworth some twenty-two "fraggers." A fragger
is a soldier who throws a fragmentation grenade into the tent
of a fellow soldier (often a superior non-commissioned or
commissioned officer), where it explodes. The Army takes
a very dim view of this; fraggers who are found guilty by a
court martial are usually sent to Leavenworth. Of the
twenty-two fraggers then at Leavenworth, twenty-one proved
to have almost classical histories of having been battered
children themselves (Bond, D., personal communication).

It is my personal belief that there is a growing amount
of violence toward children in the world, that the rising
rate of "battered child" diagnoses and criminal neglect
charges are only the tip of the iceberg, and that there is
a real effect beyond that due only to improved reporting and
more inclusive definitions. Here in the United States,
where the murder rate has nearly tripled in one generation,
and where it now stands ten times higher than in the United

Kingdom, three percent of all murders are of children murdered by their parents. It now seems reasonable to surmise
that violence toward children, including cruelty, neglect,
and other stresses related to defective family life, correlate with violent behavior by those children when they are
grown. This may well comprise a vicious cycle of increasing
violence in America that contributes to our recently sky-
rocketing statistical curves reflecting the sharp rise in
violent crime, especially since 1960. But are there not
other problems that contribute? What about poverty, for
example?

Our hypothesis (including West's Law) would appear to
require a cross-cultural experiment of nature, in which a
sizable group of people, living in great poverty, but exhibiting no cruelty, violence or neglect whatsoever toward children, would prove to have a remarkably low rate of interpersonal violence among the adults. I believe that the Tarahumara Indians provide such an example.

A Nonviolent Society of Nonviolent Families

The Tarahumara are a tribe of Mexican Indians, speaking
a Uto-Aztec language, and inhabiting the rugged Sierra Madre
mountains of southern Chihuahua and northern Sinaloa. Some
fifty-thousand in number, they are probably the least accul-
turated aboriginal group of any size remaining on the North
American continent. Relatively little is known about them in
comparison with extensively studied American and Mexican tribes
in more accessible places, although the Jesuit missionaries
have maintained friendly contact with them for generations.
However, in the past 15 years some interesting new observations
have been made (Paredes, West and Snow, 1970; Kennedy, 1978).

Archaeological data suggest that the Tarahumara Indians
have lived in the Sierra Madre Occidentale for at least 2,000
years. Their territory, some of the most broken and inhospitable terrain of North America, includes 10,000 foot peaks,
high plateaus and gigantic gorges or barrancas. The winter
climate in the uplands is the coldest in Mexico, while the
torrid summers of the deep gorges support an inhospitable
subtropical biota.

Like many other Indians of the American Southwest and
Northern Mexico, the Tarahumara are subsistence farmers.
They raise and eat corn, squash, and beans, supplemented with
a variety of wild plants and occasional fish or game. The
short growing season, scanty rainfall, organically poor soil,
and primitive agricultural techniques frequently result in
hunger, and in some years outright famine. Sheep, goats and

cattle, introduced by the Spanish, are maintained primarily
as sources of fertilizer, wool, hides, and work animals,
serving as food only upon rare, ceremonial occasions. Horses
and burros are used very little because of their cost. The
Tarahumara are extremely poor.

Many of the Tarahumara migrate annually in the fall, to
spend the winter in the shelter of the barrancas, returning
in the spring with their herds to the plateaus to plant their
corn. This unusual semi-agrarian, semi-nomadic adjustment
to an extraordinary terrain is a significant part of the
Tarahumara ecology. It may explain in part why their territory has been spared by aggressive neighbors who have not developed such an adaptational style, or who are not prepared
physically or psychologically to endure the strenuous requirements of life in the Sierra Madre.

In the uplands, the Tarahumara usually reside in small
wooden huts. At lower elevations many inhabit the numerous
caves of the barrancas. The Tarahumara settlement pattern
typically consists of one to three (usually related) family
units or rancherias that may be five miles from their near-
est neighbors. From twelve to fourteen neighboring rancherias form a pueblo, the basic socio-political unit, with an
elected gobernado (actually a judge or siriame) from within
the group. Often on Sundays and other native or Catholic
feast days, the people of a pueblo congregate at a central
site (communidad) where social, political, and religious
affairs are conducted.

While some changes are being made, most of the Tarahumara still live as did their ancestors. There is a high
infant mortality rate. While complete data are not available,
apparently a sizable majority (perhaps up to 70 or 80 percent) of the children die before the age of six, mostly of
malnutrition, infectious diseases and infestations. Pneumonia,
malaria, diphtheria, typhoid fever, and tuberculosis are still
endemic. Parasitosis is common.

The Tarahumara are careful to treat other people, including children, with great dignity. Adult couples are
never demonstrably affectionate in public, but may be so pri-
vately. These people withstand solitude easily and are seemingly untroubled by boredom. They spend many hours in thought-
ful contemplation or in keen observation of nature, with which
they are in deep harmony.

Almost every activity in Tarahumara daily life has a religious meaning. Although many have been baptized, for most

of them Christianity is only a veneer covering a core of
Indian beliefs. They believe in witchcraft. There is one
principal God, the Creator, closely identified with the Sun,
but many local deities and spirits are carefully recognized
and appeased. Dance is a form of prayer. Activities such
as drinking have a strong ritual element.

The Tarahumara mother displays considerable warmth and
affection toward her children. Much of the time she carries
the baby on her back. When she sleeps, she curls up, tucking
the child's legs between her own. Physical punishment is
never used to discipline children. Laughter at misbehavior
shames the miscreant and serves as a highly effective deter-
rent to repetition of the offense.

The Tarahumara tribal name (a Spanish corruption of
ramamuri, meaning the swift runners or fleet-of-foot) is derived from their legendary running abilities. Kick-ball
races are usually team efforts of continuous running over
broken terrain for periods of up to 72 hours (over 200 miles)
for men, 12 to 18 hours for women (who may toss a hoop with
a stick instead of kicking a ball while running), and 1 to 6
hours for children. Despite poor diet, and with little or no
training, these people may be the world's best long-distance
runners.

The Tarahumara are among the very few North American
aboriginals to have used alcohol before the white man came.
The tesguinada is their ceremonial drinking party at which
is served a native beer called tesguino made from fermented
corn sprouts and herbs. These festivals are sponsored by
individual families for their neighbors and friends, and
serve to reinforce social ties, to develop or maintain status,
and to bring in help for certain major enterprises, such as
harvesting or building, with drinking and conviviality the
only reward. In fact, social prestige among the Tarahumara
is measured to a large extent by the number, frequency, and
size of the tesguinadas a man can afford to give or is invited to attend.

In the vast and lonely reaches of the Sierra Madre, the
tesguinada provides an institution for the communication of
language, religion, mythology, customs, and a sense of tribal
identity. A man may cover more than 100 miles visiting neighbors in this "tesguino network" simply to invite them to the
party. Some measure of the role of the tesguinada in Tarahumara culture can be judged from estimates that 20 percent
of a typical family's time is used in preparing, giving, or
attending them.

<u>Tesguino</u> doesn't keep, and it will be drunk steadily
until it is gone. During this period the participants--
adult (post-pubescent) men and women--become intoxicated and
may indulge in a local saturnalia for two or three days.
However, despite this regular socially acceptable intoxication,
habitual drunkenness or chronic alcoholism is virtually unknown among the mountain Tarahumara. While it is quite
appropriate to become intoxicated during a **tesguinada**, when
much misbehavior and violations of certain taboos are tolerated, violence almost never results. This absence of alcoholism, and of alcohol-related violence, makes the Tarahumara
virtually unique among the American Indians.

The Tarahumara have great respect for the property of
others. Stealing is considered a great crime. Adultery is
usually condemned. Prostitution is not practiced. Maltreat-
ment of children is considered such a terrible crime as to
be virtually unthinkable. Suicide, which is more common among
Indians than among whites or blacks in the U.S., is essentially nonexistent among the Tarahumara. Violence of any kind,
including rape, is also virtually unknown.

Here then we have a people who are great competitors (not
only at kick-ball, but in wrestling and other sports); yet
they are scrupulously fair and honest in trade or barter.
They get drunk regularly in **tesguinadas**; nevertheless, alcoholism is not a problem. Divorce is easy, but rarely occurs;
peaceful monogamous family life is the rule. Despite des-
perate poverty these Indians do not steal.

Faced with a constant struggle for survival in a vast
wilderness, the Tarahumara are not brutal; instead they are
characterized by quiet dignity, respect for others, good
humor among themselves, and helpfulness toward strangers.

Although the frequency of minor psychophysiological
and transient neurotic syndromes keeps the shaman busy, major psychoses appear to be unusually rare in the Tarahumara.

Finally, and perhaps most remarkable of all, even though
family life is highly structured and local loyalties are
fierce, both interpersonal and intergroup violence by Tarahumara Indians are almost unknown. While much more extensive
study is obviously required, to date our inquiries reveal
the astonishing record that among these 50,000 people during
the past quarter-century there have been only one or two
homicides (essentially drunken accidents) and no suicide.

It seems likely that significant factors in the unusual
physical and mental quality of these graceful and attractive

people can be related to their ecological circumstances. The largely carbohydrate diet, with just enough protein to maintain musculature, is apparently most appropriate for long-distance runners. The great distance between families in an immense and forbidding land undoubtedly causes people to be keenly aware of their need for each other and appreciative of the value of persons.

But it is the affectionate, respectful and absolutely non-violent child-rearing practices of the Tarahumara to which the behavioral scientist's attention returns again and again. However, this leads me, in closing, to a tragic paradox. It suggests that children who never experience violence, and who are never punished (shame rather than guilt being the extinguisher of unwanted behavior) are very likely to become non-violent adults who create non-violent families.

The stability of the Tarahumara population through the centuries is obviously related to the high death rate in infancy and childhood. When only 20-30 percent of the children survive, and these children are loved, desired, and needed by parents with whom they live in close harmony in small huts or caves, the value of the child in the culture is a central and explicit matter.

Yet it is becoming obvious that modern medicine, with its prenatal care, vitamins, vaccines, antibiotics, antihelminthics, and nutritional supplements, will soon be more and more available to the Tarahumara Indians. At the same time it is clear that the culture is not geared to support larger families, and that the ecology of the Sierra Madre cannot support a population explosion. But neither the views of the influential Jesuits nor the traditions of the Tarahumara themselves would seem to make the acceptance of contraceptive practices a likely practice among them. Thus, in two generations of ten-child families, the ancient and beautiful culture of the Tarahumara could be destroyed, and the people reduced to disspirited wreckage riddled with alcoholism, obesity, diabetes, homicide, suicide, psychoses, and violence like so many of their cousins in the American Southwest. The paradox must be faced, more devastating than the famous riddle of "The Lady or The Tiger?". Should civilization rush in to save the Tarahumara babies, thereby destroying this rare and remarkable non-violent culture, or should we stand aside, as we have always done, and let them die?

References

Kennedy, J.G. 1978. Tarahumara of the Sierra Madre. Arlington Heights, Ill.: AHM Publishing Corp.

Litman, R.E., and West, L.J. 1975. Research on violence: The ethical equation. In: N. Burch and H.L. Altshuler (Eds.), Behavior and Brain Electrical Activity. New York: Plenum Publishing Corp., pp. 525-539.

MacAndrew, C. and Edgerton, R.B. 1969. Drunken Comportment: A Social Explanation. Chicago: Aldine Publishing Co. 197 pp.

Moorehead, A. 1966. The Fatal Impact: An Account of the Invasion of the South Pacific 1767-1840. London, England: Hamilton. 230 pp.

Parades, A., West, L.J., and Snow, C.C. 1970. Biosocial adaptation and correlates of acculturation in the Tarahumara ecosystem. International Journal of Social Psychiatry, 16(3):163-174.

Siciliano, S. 1961. Resulti preliminari de un indagine sull "Omicido in Danimarca." Scuola Positiva., pp. 718-29.

West. D.J. 1966. Murder Followed by Suicide. Cambridge, Mass.: Harvard University Press.

West, L.J. 1967. Psychobiology of racial violence. Archives of General Psychiatry, 16(6):645-651.

West, L.J. 1975. Psychiatric reflections on the death penalty. American Journal of Orthopsychiatry, 45(4): 689-698.

4. Functions of the Police and the Justice System in Family Violence

I am a psychologist whose research has been conducted in natural settings. My earliest involvement in such research came during ten years at Memorial/Sloan-Kettering Cancer Center in New York studying psychological adaptation to cancer and its radical surgery. During that period, my colleagues and I were fortunately able to work closely with surgeons and other medical practitioners in what we considered to be a natural stress laboratory. The hospital was a natural setting in which countless patients confronted not only the threat of a death-dealing disease but often faced surgically induced changes in body form and function as well.

Among the important lessons of that work was that while behavioral research conducted in natural environments contributed to the knowledge base, it also lent itself to quick translation of research findings to hospital procedures and to the care of patients. The gap between research and application is considerably lessened when behavioral research is conducted in collaboration with a practitioner system (Bard, 1975). In effect, both knowledge and usefulness are served simultaneously.

Police as Practitioners

For the past twelve years or so I have continued to re-fine this methodologic focus but in concert with a very different practitioner system....one uniquely concerned with the subject of this meeting. Indeed, it is inconceivable that any serious address to the subject of violence as a behavioral phenomenon can possibly exclude the police....those who serve as society's practitioners of behavior regulation.

Another of the lessons of my earlier work, as well as of my more recent activity, is that naturalistic research often requires giving up safe and familiar environments. Studying

the adaptations of the victims of physical malignancy required confronting personal discomfort in the alien world of
a cancer hospital. Similarly, the study of the social malig-
nancies of violence and crime victimization (Bard and Sangrey,
1979) has required involvement in a world of the adverse and
the perverse....with an alien practitioner system often regarded by behavioral scientists as repressive and threatening.

Police and Family Intervention

My research in collaboration with the police began in the
mid-sixties when I conceived a study to determine the feasibility of improving police effectiveness in dealing with the
perennially common and vexing problem of the family disturbance (Bard, M., 1970). For as long as there have been police,
officers have been called upon to intervene in these most
volatile of human conflicts. And there were impressive
statistics that, despite the fact that the police typically
disowned this distasteful function, it was among the most
frequent and dangerous of their tasks. In fact, about 22%
of police deaths occurred while intervening as a third-party
in disputes, often among family members. About 40% of police
injuries occurred in the same way.

As for the public, there was ample evidence that homicide and assault were related to intimacy. Family members
and friends were responsible for from 50% to 80% of homicide
victims, dependent on geographic location. Typically, family
disputes were "resolved" by the temporary expedient of an
arrest....often an empty gesture since, when passions sub-
sided, the complainant frequently dropped the charge.

In conceiving the project I hypothesized that a planned
association between psychologists and police officers would
result in a mix of insight and skill that would have some
ameliorative effect on the problem. If nothing else, interpersonal skill and competence specific to conflict management might reduce injuries and deaths to both officers and
citizens. In addition, there was a hope that the police
could serve an early warning or case-finding function as a
preventive mental health measure....a concept just gaining
currency in the mid-sixties.

However, my colleagues and I were concerned about
possibly confusing the officers as to their identity. Could
we give them the skills usually associated with social science
and the clinical professions and yet keep their identities as
police officers intact? Could we avoid making them over in
our own image....the common pit-fall in the consultant role?

The risk here was very real, by confusing the officers we might endanger them....that is, by inhibiting their normal survival-oriented alertness.

Demonstration Study

After an intensive period of training, a selected group of 18 officers operated as generalist-specialists in one precinct of New York City with a population of about 90,000. In a period of 21 months the officers intervened in 1,388 disturbances that took place in 962 families. The results of the study were encouraging: 1) there were no assaults upon any of the 18 officers despite a statistical probability that there would be; 2) there were no homicides during the study period in any family known to the officers; 3) there was a reduction in family assaults; 4) the officers made targeted referrals to a range of social and mental health agencies while the few referrals made by the comparison precinct were mostly to Family Court; and, 5) there was the impression of a favorable community response.

While the findings were promising, demonstration studies often raise as many questions as they answer. Consequently, following Campbell and Stanley (1963), a quasi-experimental study was designed and was undertaken with the police of the New York City Housing Authority. Introducing elements of control that were not possible in the initial feasibility study, the second research was conducted in three public housing projects over a one-year period. In addition to confirming the findings of the original demonstration, we determined that officers trained in conflict management were measurably superior in all police performance than were officers who were not specially trained (Zacker and Bard, 1973).

But for whatever advantages these two studies had for the police and for the people with whom they deal, the most fascinating prospect was in the opportunity for acquiring new knowledge about behavior. At the very least, the two studies offered an opportunity to examine questions about interpersonal conflict and about violence. Three issues were particularly intriguing. The conventional wisdom of the police holds 1) that they are called to family disputes because of assaultiveness or the threat of physical assault; 2) that alcohol is likely to be a causative factor in the dispute; and, 3) that assaultiveness is likely to be causally associated with alcohol use.

Interestingly, the view that alcohol and violence are causally related is also shared by social scientists. For

example, Wolfgang and Ferracuti (1967), in their comprehensive review on violence, while acknowledging that in most
cases alcohol does not result in violence, nevertheless consistently refer to a paired association between the two.
Others (Brecher, 1972) have noted that alcohol appears to
play a causative role in homicide, suicide, automobile fatal-
ities and other violence-related behavior. Experimental
laboratory studies of both animals and humans have also tended to infer causal relationships even when findings have been
ambiguous (Shuntich and Taylor, 1972).

Our studies presented an opportunity for systematic
naturalistic observation of human conflict which could be
presumed to be violent-prone since police intervention was
required. We discovered, to our surprise, that the presumption was incorrect. In analyzing data on 1,388 cases (Bard
and Zacker, 1974) we found that assaultiveness was involved
in fewer than one third of the incidents. If, as we suspect,
the police are called mostly to assure an immediately available and objective third-party to bring about a constructive
outcome, then officers expecting violence may inadvertently
behave in ways to make it happen.

Also, we found that family disputes are not usually influenced by alcohol use. In fewer than half of the cases
had at least one of the parties used alcohol. Indeed, even
where alcohol had been used, many were judged by the officers
as having been sober. Admittedly there were no tests employed to determine alcohol blood volume or cognitive and affective measures made of the effects of alcohol. But police
officers are astute observers of behavior....their observational skills having survival value....their specially trained judgments are presumed to be meaningful in this large
sample, particularly since a reliability check was used.

Alcohol and Violence

However, the most surprising and perhaps profound finding....one that certainly warrants further investigation....
assaults were less common when alcohol had been used. Given
laboratory evidence of the disinhibiting effects of alcohol
on aggressive impulses, this was quite unexpected. In fact,
analysis of the coincidence of assault and alcohol use, indicates that alcohol was less likely to have been used in
assaultive disputes than in non-assaultive disputes.

By the way, we did have more than casual interest in
what we could learn about the prediction of violence. In the
three studies, with a total of more than 2,000 cases, we have
found support for Mischel's observation (1973) that past

behavior tends to be the best single predictor of future behavior. Consistently, the best predictor of violence in our
studies was a history of violent behavior.

Once again let me emphasize that these findings were derived from data collected by those whose normal functions
positioned them in time and in place to deal with conflict
and violence. In effect, the design of the original demonstration and the subsequent quasi-experiment permitted police
officers to function as social science investigators while
performing their routine tasks. However, data collection
requirements refined the nature of their observations and
added dimension to observational skills. In both studies
debriefing of the officers served to further enrich the
data and to permit reliability checks. The prospect of having
specially trained police officers participate in research on
conflict and violence strikes me as having at least as much
validity as, for example, having bedside physicians participate in clinical research on the lymphomas.

In building this model there were obvious issues still
to be addressed. Both of the studies were concerned with
family disputes....would other kinds of disputes provide
similar outcomes? Would results be the same if the data was
collected in a small city with a normal ethnic and socioeconomic distribution as in the ethnically homogeneous and
working class large inner city community of the first two
studies? These questions, among others, were addressed by
the conduct of a third study in the city of Norwalk,
Connecticut (Bard and Zacker, 1976)....in an effort to determine how police officers, not specially trained in methods
of third-party intervention, typically intervene in interpersonal conflicts.

That study did not restrict itself to family disputes.
Rather, all conflict situations for which police intervention was sought were considered within the purview of the
study....landlord-tenant disputes; neighbor disputes; store-
keeper-customer disputes; as well as family disputes. In a
rather complex design, officers participating in the study
systematically observed and recorded their own behaviors as
well as the behaviors of others in conflict situations. One
of the objectives in the study was to evaluate, define and
classify third-party approaches to interpersonal conflict.

The Norwalk study had as its major focus the establish-
ment of a practitioner-researcher coupling mechanism to gain
understanding of a singularly important aspect of interpersonal behavior. By focusing on interpersonal processes
we found that police officers, without formal training,

improved their perceptions of interpersonal processes, increased their knowledge of human behavior and appropriately altered their own behavior. The basic means for achieving this change, the use of a self-report form and the debriefing process used for the purposes of research, appears to have had an important educational value.

Naturally we were interested as well in determining the role of physical assaultiveness and the use of alcohol in the 344 general interpersonal disputes studied in Norwalk. The results of this study (Zacker and Bard, 1977) confirmed our previous findings: physical assaultiveness was not usually a factor in interpersonal disputes when the police arrived; that interpersonal disputes managed by the police were not usually influenced by alcohol use; and, that assaultiveness was not related to alcohol use in such disputes. Because the study was conducted in a more heterogeneous environment and with a broad range of disputes, we were able to confirm that assaultiveness is more likely in close relationships than in distant relationships or between strangers. This supports the long-recognized association between violence and intimacy. Also, assaultiveness appears to be associated with poverty rather than with race; and finally, it is as likely in a largely middle class city as in a poor inner city community.

We have found that intervention in family disputes is a police function that is feared and disliked by those who perform it, needed but resented by those who receive it, and often greatly misunderstood by society at large. Yet, in a highly mobile society like ours, where the extended family is no longer available as a here-and-now resource, there remains a need for external control over runaway emotions and behaviors. Whereas families once relied on a respected relative or friend to exercise authority or contain an emotionally charged situation that threatened to escalate out of control, they now rely on the police.

Criteria for Police Intervention

When do the police become involved? In most cases, the police are called to the scene of a family fight by one of the disputing parties; in some instances they are summoned by a neighbor or passer-by. Families whose fights receive police attention are disproportionately poor and of minority background. Sometimes, the appeal to the police follows an assault; more often, however, they are called not because a crime has been committed, but because one of the parties becomes afraid that things are getting out of hand. There are

only two studies reporting data specific to police-managed
family disputes. In one (Bard & Zacker, 1974) there was
evidence of assault in 29% of 1,388 cases. In the other
(Zacker & Bard, 1977) there were assaults in 44% of 148
disputes between relatives. However, neither study was restricted to disputes between spouses; 15% of the former
sample and 20% of the latter, the disputes were between
parents and their (usually adolescent) children.

A call to the police can be seen as a constructive act,
an attempt to prevent or break the escalation of violence.
No statistically sophisticated incidence projections exist
for intrafamilial violence in the population as a whole. However, simple inspection of existing figures suggests that
more victims of spouse abuse do not call the police than do.
Moreover, families who ask the police for help may be quite
different from those who suffer assault in silence. Thus,
although police practice in cases of wife abuse has properly
come under scrutiny, it should be noted that improvement in
this area is likely to represent only a partial solution to
that particular problem.

Techniques of Intervention

What do police do when they intervene in a family dispute? There have been only a few observational studies of
police behavior in family disputes, but their findings are
consistent with one another as well as with officers' informal accounts of routine practice (Bard & Zacker, 1976;
Parnas, 1967; Reiss, 1973; Stephens, 1977). After gaining
entry, police will generally separate the disputants, check
to see that no weapons or potential weapons are available,
and try to find out from each spouse what happened. If
necessary, they will administer first aid or summon medical
assistance. They may also arrange to have children or other
non-disputants leave the immediate setting. The purpose of
the investigation is to determine whether or not a law has
been violated and what action is appropriate. Most accounts
of police practice agree that when serious injuries have
occurred to give the officer probable cause for an arrest
and/or when a victim insists on signing a complaint, the
officer is likely to exercise the arrest option. (Reiss,
1973; Stephens, 1977; Parnas, 1967). However, the same
sources also agree that arrest is a less certain outcome
when the victim and assailant are related than when they are
strangers.

The content, as distinct from the general approach of
police intervention, depends on the circumstances of the dis-

pute, the motivation, background and training of the officer,
the policies of the police department and the laws and
resources of the community. Should insufficient grounds exist
for an immediate arrest, police may refer a complainant to
court to seek a restraining order or warrant. At other times
they may order one of the parties, usually the husband, out of
the house. They may take a woman and her children to an
emergency shelter if one exists. They may refer a disputing
couple to a marriage counselor or an appropriate social
service agency. They may discourage a complainant from in-
sisting on prosecution by explaining the time and likely outcomes involved in court proceedings.

Role of Arrest and Prosecution

In the majority of family disputes, the police do not
regard arrest as the most desirable solution. It is society's
most drastic form of behavior regulation and its object is
punishment rather than correction. In addition, more often
than not, it initiates a judicial process with little chance
of a satisfactory outcome. According to a task force report to the National Commission of the Causes and Prevention
of Violence (Campbell et al, 1970):

> "the yardstick for testing the application of a
> mature, sensitive understanding and coolheaded-
> ness is often (once deciding that intervention
> is necessary) how quickly and quietly a patrol-
> man can restore calm without having to make an
> arrest. This is what 'good cops' are made of.
> This is what constitutes 'good police work.'
> This is what breeds community respect for the
> police (p. 302-303)."

In individual cases, an officer may dissuade a victim
of family violence from prosecuting his or her spouse because of personal bias, misinformation, or a cynical unwillingness to invest the time and energy involved in processing
an arrest. Indeed, there are times when taking custody of a
violent person may be the only available method of ensuring
a family's safety. When an officer fails to act under such
circumstances he or she is in error, and should be held
accountable.

For the most part, however, policies and practices
which encourage officers to seek alternatives to arrest are
consistent both with progressive legal thought and with the
practical realities of invoking the criminal process. Our
courts are overcrowded, understaffed, and unable to process

the increasing numbers of offenders brought to them each year.
Thus, when a family dispute is referred to court it may be
days or weeks before any action is taken - ample time for
fights either to escalate or to be forgotten. Should action
be taken, "correction" through criminal sanction does little,
if anything, to improve the family relationship. If spouses
choose to divorce or separate this may not matter; if they do
not, the consequences of having invoked the criminal process
ultimately may be destructive. A practical consideration for
police officers is the fact that, in American communities, a
person arrested in a family dispute (as for many other crimes)
rather than being held until a court appearance, is released
almost immediately after posting a small bond or simply signing a statement agreeing to come to court to respond to the
charges. Once arrested and released, a spouse not only has
limited incentive to stop fighting but, in fact, now has a
new grievance.

Police arrest practices are usually different for assault
cases occurring within families than for those between
strangers. In the former, the aggrieved may be tied economically and socially to the accused. What is more, it is very
difficult to engage in routine family life activities while
the emotional and financial strains associated with adver-
sary court proceedings are pending. Given the psychological
and economic realities, it is understandable that victims
drop charges once the violent spouse has "cooled down."
Police disillusionment with the efficacy of arrest in such
cases is based upon repeated experience with the "dropped
charge syndrome." Some question the police perception; they
contend that there is no evidence that charges are dropped
any more in family-related complaints than in any other
crimes (Martin, 1977). The limited data that do exist, however, support informal police perceptions. Reiss (1973)
analyzed statistics from Chicago collected during 1966.
Assault (of which 65% of the cases involved relatives or
neighbors) was the only major index crime for which the
clearance rate due to victim's failure to prosecute (32%)
was higher than the clearance rate by arrest (28%).

The complexity of the family dispute as a category of
interaction and the seriousness of the consequences result-
ing from mismanagement make it evident that the police
function in such matters needs refinement and improvement.
What the police currently do is not enough. Stephens (1977)
reported data from a Kansas City, Missouri, analysis of
serious assaults and homicides within families. In 85% of
the cases, police had responded to a disturbance call at the
victim's and/or suspect's address at least once in the prior

two years.   In 49.7% of the cases, they had visited five or
more times.   The effectiveness of these opportunities to
prevent future violence is a tragic reminder of the need for
change.

Refusal of Police Help

However, even with the most effective intervention
strategy, a real dilemma may arise (Bard & Zacker, 1971).There
are those rare instances when the interaction between the disputing parties leads to a prediction of a dire outcome and
yet both parties remain resistant to help.   Regardless of the
potential danger, the parties have the Constitutional right
to refuse help.   Indeed, the individual right to liberty has
precedence over a behavioral prediction.   Violence prevention outreach programs must acknowledge such dilemmas and
operate as effectively as possible within their constraints.
The principles which govern such interventions may require
highly sophisticated adaptations in the shadowy interface
between psychology and the law.

Public Policy Implications[1]

Police policy in relation to family disturbances had
undergone important changes during the past decade.   The
major development is the acknowledgement that force and
criminal sanction are insufficient means for managing disturbed family relationships requiring police intervention.
The traditional police view was that conflict is an evil
which must be repressed if order is to be preserved; the
more advanced police view is that conflict is inevitable
(particularly in intimate relationships) and that it can have
constructive potentials.

Criticisms of Police

At the same time that the police have been seeking to
improve their methods of managing violent family encounters,
organized criticism of their response to instances of wife
abuse has been escalating.   In substance, criticisms have
focused on the following issues (Field and Lehman, 1977;
Martin, 1977; Roy, 1977):

1) that the police tend to regard family disputes
   as private "civil matters" rather than as
   criminal violations subject to arrest;

---

[1]This discussion is abstracted from Bard, M. and Connolly, H.
The Police and Family Violence: Policy and Practice. U.S.
Commission on Civil Rights, 1978.

2) that the police downgrade the importance of these altercations and instead give higher priority to those events they regard as being "real" police work;

3) that the police are likely to disbelieve a woman who complains about her partner's abuse;

4) that the police response is a reflection of the negative personal predilections of individual officers; i.e., that most officers are sexist, inept, lazy and/or uncaring.

I cannot deny that cases exist to validate these criticisms; obviously, they do. However, I question the simplistic remedies proposed. The central point in all of this is the question of police discretion and, with respect to this important issue, two opposing philosophies exist: 1) advocates for battered women propose severe limitations on the discretionary authority of police who intervene in family disputes. In essence, they demand that the police arrest any man accused of assaulting his female partner and that in such cases the police be prohibited from discouraging arrest or offering to mediate; 2) those who propose maintaining the latitude provided by broad discretion assert that the most satisfactory improvement in police response would be caused by an increase in the sophistication and range of options available to officers managing family conflicts.

Controversy on Limits of Police Discretion

Those who seek to limit discretion have chosen a course that essentially blames police practitioners for their failures, whether these failures are personal or are reflections of larger social or cultural values. In effect, to limit discretion is to tacitly "punish" all officers for the bad performance of some. This kind of attribution is not only morally tinged but it implies that the practitioner's competence cannot be improved. It assumes further that unsatisfactory practitioner performance can be eliminated by the simple expedient of designing a formula to ensure that all family offense complainants are facilitated in seeking a legal or judicial remedy. Obviously, this ideal is untenable in a system which, of necessity, handles a wide variety of situations requiring different actions, and which functions with limited administrative and supervisory control over individual police-citizen encounters. Finally, those who advocate limiting discretion make the additional assumption that invoking the judicial process will best ensure the rights of battered women. A questionable assumption at best.

The opposing position contends that improvement of police knowledge, skills and personal satisfaction are the most effective means for improving the service provided battered women, as well as all others whose "family disputes" come to police attention. It assumes further that the expectation of responsible behavior breeds responsible behavior. Finally, because family disputes are complicated and may differ greatly from one another, discretion is believed essential to the preservation of citizen's rights:

> "The exercise of administrative discretion
> with appropriate legislative guidance and
> subject to appropriate review and control
> is likely to be more protective of basic
> rights than the routine, uncritical appli-
> cation by police of rules of law which are
> often necessarily vague or overgeneralized
> in their language (President's Commission
> on Law Enforcement and Administration of
> Justice, 1964)."

From this perspective, the protection of the "rights" of battered women consists not simply of legal access, but of achieving a functional match between each woman's unique needs and the resources made available by society. To be sure, in practice this would sometimes consist of arrest and the application of legal sanctions. At other times, it would mean other kinds of help more appropriate to the circumstances that exist at the time of the intervention.

Hazards to Police

Intervening in family disputes always has involved hazards for police officers, both physically and emotionally. Injuries and deaths of officers in these circumstances attest to the danger involved. But less well understood is the source of frustration inherent in these events. No two family disturbances are exactly alike; there are always subtle but important differences among them. For the person who must manage them, they are all similarly frustrating, incredibly complex and doggedly resistant to solution. Even under the best of circumstances, with psychiatric, legal or social work intervention and with spouses who are intelligent, well educated and economically secure, the powerful emotions at play create intractable obstacles that are almost impossible to overcome.

Tragic Outcomes of "Protection" by Arrest

In the past, many male officers were burdened also by the value-derived dilemma of "protecting the little woman."

In these instances arrest was often the option employed as officers demonstrated their power to protect the "weaker sex" against the depredations of a brutal spouse. The outcomes of such gallantry were sometimes tragic. At times the outraged husband or lover would retaliate for "loss of face" by further violence directed against the woman or some police officer. Or, in some instances, the officer's efforts to protect by force or arrest would provoke the woman to ally herself with the man against the officer, now defined as the common enemy. Such experiences were, in part, responsible for a growing disinclination to use the arrest option except where absolutely necessary. In fact, many programs of training in family crisis intervention consider a decrease in arrest for family-related offenses to be an indication of success.

On the other hand, there are many police officers who long for the simple solution that the arrest option offers. Because of their action orientation and their intolerance for delay in "doing something," the intangible quality of negotiation or mediation can be disturbing. They would prefer simple and direct action in dealing with what they perceive as misconduct and injustice. For these officers, resorting to "the law" has simple, direct action imperatives which they see as getting them out of the "social work business." So, in many ways, the pressure for reform, which requires resorting to a judicial remedy, has the effect of moving the police system back to its traditional position of enforcing compliance rather than in serving to potentiate the constructive possibilities in a dispute. Strange as it may seem, the proponents of limiting police discretion in family disputes appear to crave the simple, direct and uncomplicated solution as much as do traditionally oriented police officers.

Conclusion

Of all systems of government, over time, the police have had the most sustained, immediate and direct exposure to disturbed families. These troubled relationships are unpredictable and highly volatile; they defy even the most skilled intervention. Responding to family disturbances comprises a significant part of police working time. While fewer than half of the cases are in any way violent, the function cannot be delegated to any other system because of the latent violence in them and because of the possible need for invoking the criminal sanction.

In any case, the police system would appear to have unique potentials for dealing with family disturbances and for preventing the violence which sometimes occurs in them. Police practitioners are immediately available as a resource and have the real as well as symbolic authority to do something here-and-now, when emotions are at their height.

What police officers do has become the focus of interest for those who seek to ensure the rights of battered women. Some have contended that the best way of ensuring those rights is to limit the discretion of individual police so that they must invariably inform family offense complainants of the legal remedies available. Others have argued that wife beating and family disputes are not synonomous and that the best approach to the problem is to preserve police discretion but to reinforce it by methods that improve practitioner skill and competence.

Our analysis has led us to conclude that the latter position is, on balance, the most realistic. We are concerned, however, about the serious inadequacies in the data base available for reasoned judgments. Well-intentioned reforms can be self-defeating if public policy changes rest solely on egregious case reasoning. It is our conviction that any changes mandated in police management of family disputes be based upon objective data available only through the conduct of sound research. To do otherwise may serve the purposes of advocacy well, but do unnecessary mischief in the lives of people.

References

Bard, M. Training police as specialists in family crisis intervention. National Institute of Law Enforcement and Criminal Justice, Washington, D.C.: U.S. Government Printing Office, 1970 (monograph).

Bard, M. & Zacker, J. The prevention of family violence: dilemmas of community intervention. Journal of Marriage and the Family, Nov. 1971, 677-682.

Bard, M. & Zacker, J. Assaultiveness and alcohol use in family disputes: police perceptions. Criminology, 1974, 12 (3), 281-292.

Bard, M. Collaboration between law enforcement and the social sciences. Professional Psychology, 1975, 6 (2), 127-134.

Bard, M. and Zacker, J. The Police and Interpersonal Conflict: Third Party Intervention Approaches. Washington, D.C., Police Foundation, 1976 (monograph).

Bard, M. and Connally, H. The Police and Family Violence: Policy and Practice. U.S. Civil Rights Commission, Washington, D.C. 1978.

Bard, M. and Sangrey, D. The Crime Victim's Book. New York: Basic Books, 1979.

Brecher, E.M. Licit and Illicit Drugs. Mt. Vernon, N.Y.: Consumers Union, 1972.

Campbell, D. and Stanley, J. Experimental and quasi-experimental designs for research on teaching. In: N. Gage (Ed.) Handbook for Research on Teaching. Chicago: Rand McNally and Co., 1963.

Campbell, J., Sahid, J. and Stang, D. Law and order reconsidered: Report of the Task Force on Law and Law Enforcement to the National Commission on the Causes and Prevention of Violence. N.Y.: Bantam Books, 1970.

Fields, M. and Lehman, E. A handbook for beaten women. N.Y. Brooklyn Legal Services Corp. 1977.

Martin, D. Battered Wives. N.Y.: Pocket Books, 1977.

Mischel, W. Toward a cognitive social learning reconceptualization of personality. Psychological Review, 80, 1973, 252-283.

Parnas, R. The police response to the domestic disturbance. Wisconsin Law Review, 1967, n.2.

President's Commission on Law Enforcement and Administration of Justice, Task Force Report: the police, Washington, D.C.: U.S. Government Printing Office, 1967.

Reiss, A. Policing everyday life. In Sweeney, T. and Ellingsworth, W. (Eds.) Issues in police patrol: a book of readings. Washington, D.C.: Kansas City, Missouri Police Department and The Police Foundation, 1973, 82-128.

Roy, M. (Ed.). Battered Women: A psychosociological study of domestic violence. N.Y.: Van Nostrand, 1977.

Shuntich, R.J. and Taylor, S.P. The effects of alcohol on human agression. Journal of Experimental Research on Personality, 6, 1972, 34-38.

Stephens, D. Domestic assault: the police response. In
    Roy, M. (Ed.), Battered Women. N.Y.: Van Nostrand,
    1977, 164–172.

Wolfgang, M. and Ferracuti, F. The Sub-Culture of Violence.
    London: Tavistock, 1967.

Zacker, J. and Bard, M. Effects on conflict management
    training upon police performance. Journal of Applied
    Psychology, 2, 1973, 202–208.

Zacker, J. and Bard, M. Further findings on assaultiveness
    and alcohol use in interpersonal disputes. American
    Journal of Community Psychology, 1977, 5, (4), 373–383.

Discussion

As a police administrator and as a practitioner, I want to emphasize the practical application of Dr. Bard's theories. I studied with Dr. Bard and applied his valuable research to my work in Columbus, Georgia. This is a town with a population of 250,000 people and 400 employees in its municipal police department.

Municipal police are unique among law enforcement agencies for the broad range of authority they possess and services they offer. However, they have not been adequately prepared for their community role. They have been encouraged to have a false image of themselves as typified by Starsky and Hutch on T.V. Unfortunately, this is reinforced by the fact that most of the public has the same false image, seeing only "Good Guys" and "Bad Guys." In fact, crime fighting represents less than 30% of the activities of police in general.

Police officers frequently become disillusioned, developing a sense of painful inadequacy with social problems, conflict management and crisis intervention. In Columbus, less than 20% of 2,000 calls in 1978 related to criminal violence; the remainder were non-criminal situations--people in trouble seeking help from their police department. In these cases, the police are mainly involved with products of breakdown of the social order in the form of civil disputes and family disturbances. Nonetheless, the duty is perilous--175 police officers were killed trying to resolve family disputes.

Aside from the danger posed by domestic violence, many police officers, inadequately prepared for this duty, feel helpless and inadequate and thus inappropriately invoke criminal justice, thereby compounding the problem they have encountered. It is an old saying that physicians bury their

mistakes, military tacticians classify them and police
officers arrest theirs.

Within the past decade administrators have begun to respond to these problems by developing conflict management
techniques and practice. With the help of the pioneering
work of Morton Bard, police have now developed a reservoir of
knowledge and skills, making social services an essential
part of police training. As Dr. Bard first pointed out, the
police have a unique potential for crisis management; they
are usually the only community agency available 24 hours a
day, seven days a week.

In 1974, with the help of training from Dr. Bard and a
grant, we set up a training program for the entire police
force of Columbus, Georgia. On the research end, we studied
the effect of training on the police officers and the effect
of the training program on the community. The training was
done through 64 hours of classroom teaching with the use of
role-playing techniques and videotape. Classroom skits and
little theater were used to imitate actual events. In addition, special training was provided in the use of non-verbal
skills for more effective intervention and far greater safety. Much resistance was encountered, both from within the
police force and from the community, but with patient, per-
sistent explanation and effort, the program eventually was
received very well by the police, the community and the cli-
entele serviced.

5. Conclusion

If the Houston symposium had produced no other result, it would have been valuable, I think, in puncturing certain widely held alarmist assumptions concerning the extent and nature of violence in the American family.

The "epidemic" of violence of which we heard so much would seem, on the evidence, to have been largely an appearance, a Chicken Little interpretation of statistics that in themselves reflect nothing more alarming than improved sampling and the lessened social tolerance of brute force as an instrument in the disciplining of children, the resolution of domestic crises, and the perpetuation of the paternal autocracy. No doubt the statistics also reflect the new egalitarian consciousness of both women and children, their demands for personal dignity and self-determination. Now they are fighting back, on the most literal level, and the new violence of rebellion draws an attention that was never accorded the accepted old violence of repression.

Again on the evidence, familial violence seems not to be significantly pathological, neurological, nor idiosyncratic. It is, as Dr. Straus demonstrates, "normal," given the implicit and asserted values of our society, its contradictions, and the social and situational factors that seem to precipitate most domestic explosions.

But one must not minimize the change that has taken place in extrafamilial violence: murder by strangers has increased twice as fast as murder by relatives, friends and acquaintances. It has more than tripled in Chicago from 1965 to 1973. In 1967 one-half of all rapes were committed by estranged husbands, lovers, relatives and friends; in 1975, two-thirds of all rapes were committed by strangers. Robbers only injured one victim out of five in 1967; in 1975 they in-

jured one victim out of three.   Robbery killings now occur
five times as frequently as they did in the 1960's.

Has the all-pervasive, powerful influence of television,
with its constant flow of violent images, its apparent in-
citement to violence, actually, significantly affected the
incidence or the character of domestic violence?   On the face
of it, one would suppose so.   Common sense tells us that the
constant exposure to luridly dramatized mayhem and murder
must inevitably produce pernicious results--and that is exactly what earlier investigators felt with regard to the
penny dreadful, the dime novel, the pulp Western, the gang-
ster film.   Investigation does not validate--or has not yet
validated--this conclusion.   As we have seen, no direct causal
relationship has yet been demonstrated between television
fantasy and violent behavior on the part of its juvenile audience.   Possible exception: the "background" of the unattend-
ed television set, left blatting all day in the home, does
seem to heighten the aggressive tendencies of children.   And
the distracting, energy-taxing, meaningless static of the
television set jangles their nerves.   A small minority of
particularly vulnerable children are encouraged to increase
their violent behavior by some television shows.   Hence, as
the Singers and Friedrich-Cofer have indicated, there should
be further efforts to moderate this influence, on behalf of
children, as many European countries have already done.

Ethnic and other sub-cultural variables make for differences in the incidence, character, and definition of domestic
violence, as any oldtime urban policeman could have told us--
and as our literature, film, and television do tell us constantly.   We live in a heterogeneous society, and ought to be
more aware of it by now.   Occasionally someone makes a mis-
take: a man is arrested on a street corner for "violent and
disorderly" conduct, and it develops that he was only shout-
ing and waving his arms in friendly debate, in the accustomed
manner of his Hispanic neighbors.   So with households.   There
is violence and there is "violence," and caseworkers learn to
distinguish one from the other.

In the mainstream tradition, no policeman was ever known
to respond to the cries of a boy being escorted to the woodshed by an angry father.   By the same token, the astute "cop
on the beat" relied on an informed and accurate appraisal of
actual threat to life, limb, and social order in deciding
whether to intervene in any domestic crisis.   It is only since
the intervenor has become a stranger in uniform, unfamiliar
with the ways of the people in his patrol car sector, that
special training in domestic intervention has become necessary.

Times change, the woodshed is obsolete, and so is the foot patrolman. The cross-cultural comparisons described so well by Dr. John Spiegel and Dr. Louis Jolyon West are extremely important in their imperative implication that we take pains to understand every incident of violence not only from the unique individual circumstances but also from the specific characteristics of the ethnic group. Most people have some notion of this, but the popular stereotypes held by the police and unsophisticated laymen are inadequate to the understanding required. Dr. Spiegel is attempting to remedy this by teaching ethnopsychiatry to medical students, psychiatric residents and other related professions.

Dr. West's exciting contribution is especially important for pointing the way, long hoped for, toward minimizing violence by making it shameful in our early child education, media, and literature. Although it runs against the grain of our entire Western culture, it raises a banner of hope that many might rally to.

In coping with the social reality, generalizations are of little help: we must look to what is actually happening now, and weigh the particularities of the case in the context of both the sub-culture and the wider society.

I am inclined, personally, to accept the Straus verdict on the largely social-situational nature of violence in the family. At the same time, I must concede an important practical point to Dr. Bloch: violence is a continuum, encompassing varying degrees of loosely "acceptable" force at one end and decidedly unacceptable levels—child abuse, mayhem, maiming, murder—at the other, and we must draw a strong, clear line somewhere, without too much niggling about causes. By all means let us examine the society, the ground from which violence arises. Then let us consider the unacceptable anomalies, and how best to deal with them.

Americans are a violent people, ours is a violent society. So goes the cliché. We admit it. In fact, we accept it with a glib readiness that renders it almost a boast. Try substituting some other pejorative adjective, such as cowardly, venal, flabby, obtuse. They don't go down at all well, do they?

The fact is that we feel subtly flattered by the "violent" tag. We wear it with equanimity because it seems to touch the roots of our strength and manliness; it suggests that we are formidable. We are no more disturbed by it than an Irishman is to be told of his "Irish temper." We are rather proud of our temper.

In the scale of primary human values--American values
and those of most other nations, too--strength is supreme
and violence is implicit in it. If the meek inherit, they
will do it later, when numbers and dawning consciousness
have made them stronger. Force commands respect, assures
dominance, seizes the lion's share of worldly goods, and is
understood to be our ultimate insurance against disgrace,
subjection, or annihilation. Force guarantees treaties, establishes boundaries, guards frontiers; no crucial clash of
will or interest among tribes or nations has ever been resolved, in the final analysis, in any other fashion than by
force or the threat of it; no nation has ever relinquished
any important advantage for sweet reason. The repeating
rifle in the hands of a rapidly expanding population made
American destiny manifest to the tribes and pueblos. We had
it, they did not.

To say this is to belabor the obvious: any child knows
it without need to articulate it. But that is precisely the
point. That is the social background. Virtually everything
in a dominant, aggressive society--schools, texts, the mass
media, casual entertainment, business, sports, social rank-
ings, sexual competition, our wars, picketline confronta-
tions, prisons, the policeman's idly swinging club and ready
revolver--daily and hourly affirm the lesson that might is
right. We grow up with it as a fundamental assumption, like
gravity.

The spillover is violence: we call it violence when it
is unacceptable, we voice alarm when it breaches the implicit terms of the social contract, upsets accustomed agree-
able or profitable arrangements, when the unhappy workers
set fire to the factory or stone their replacements, when the
pupils jostle the teacher, when the youngster whose ears were
boxed seizes the breadknife. We call it violence when it is
unsanctioned, when it seems destructive of the larger social
purpose, of the order on which efficient production depends,
when it threatens to sap the strength or challenges the
licit force of the society. We condemn it, too, when it of-
fends the general sense of propriety and morality, when it
challenges accepted values.

I am not, by any means, attempting to explain away a
social problem by examining causes and juggling definitions.
Rather, I am seeking to establish the basis for a set of use-
ful distinctions to be made between behavior that is rooted
in the language, customs, and deep, scarcely conscious fundamental assumptions of the society, and unacceptable anomalies
of behavior that can be governed, treated, or extirpated.

The assumption of force as the ultimate arbiter of right is deeply and universally held. Note Dr. Straus:

> . . . a great deal of family violence occurs be-
> cause men grow up thinking they have the right
> to the final say in family matters. Yet . . .
> many men lack the greater economic resources
> and superior personal qualities needed to jus-
> tify such privileges.

Does Dr. Straus suggest that the possession of greater resources and superior personal qualities would justify the use of force in establishing a man's right to "the final say"? Probably not, but I suspect that many men would draw precisely that inference. Force captures the glittering prizes, and violence in the service of right is deemed right.

Beyond the question of basic assumptions, it should be noted in passing that we tend to <u>enjoy</u> violence, to be pleasurably stimulated by it when it is not personally threatening. That is, we enjoy conflict as a spectacle, from boxing match to bull ring. Small surprise that some families should engage in it with a degree of pleasure, and make up happily afterwards.

(In this same connection, it is interesting to observe that the most popular of violent television shows, by far, are those of the "police action" genre. The reason, no doubt, is that a double satisfaction is offered. The viewer's power fantasies are indulged in identification with a protagonist who exterminates social vermin with boot, fist, and blazing pistol. Rough justice is done, just as the viewer himself would like to do it. And at the same time, social order is assured. The violence is <u>licit</u>, the exterminator is a <u>licensed</u> killer. Thus the formula allays the very anxiety that its violence creates.)

It would seem, then, that "normal" violence is both a human propensity and a side-effect of lifelong conditioning, particularly marked in a dominant, aggressive society such as our own. It occurs both in conformity with the prevailing mores, as "acceptable" violence, e.g., the use of moderate force in the disciplining of children, and in reflexive emotional response to situational frustration. It also occurs in the course of the collisions that inevitably accompany rapid social change, a fact that accounts for much of the violence that we are presently experiencing, both in the home and elsewhere.

To recognize this much can be helpful to the extent that it enables us to draw the line of which I have spoken, and to distinguish the background violence about which we can do little or nothing as individuals from the violent fallout of social upheaval and the aberrant violence that directly concerns us as therapists, caseworkers, forensic specialists, social scientists.

I think it is important to make accurate assessments in individual areas and cases, and to observe instances of social change with great care. For example, much has been written about the turmoil of the public schools and the unruly character of present-day pupils in urban areas. No one seems to take note of the striking fact that many or most of the violent pupils of today--rapists, robbers, addicts terrorizing teachers--would not have been in school in a more tranquil, earlier era. They would have joined the work force before they had attained the physical growth or reached the level of frustration that make them a menace today. This should not be understood as the explanation for school violence. That is a complex subject in itself, which has much to do with the general issues already raised, the specific problems of inner-city deterioration and the destructive, alienating impact of the current welfare system.

Studies of individuals who have come to the attention of legal or medical authorities because of outbreaks of violence in the home or the community have helped to draw a profile of the aberrant--but not always pathological--offender. Warning signs include confusion concerning sexual identity, feelings of impotence, high-level frustration, marked social or generational isolation, and, in the case of women as well as men, a sense of entrapment in which violence seems the only way out.

There is, obviously, a great deal more to be learned before we can begin to deal effectively with the multi-faceted problem of violence in the family. To begin to see the problem clearly is in itself a long step forward, and I think the Houston symposium has made a positive contribution toward that end.

Index

abuse
  child, *see* child abuse
  parental, *see* parents
  spouse, *see* spouse abuse
  wife, *see* wife abuse
achievement, personal, as
  cause of aggressive/
  violent behavior, 59,
  85. *See also* aggression
action/adventure television
  shows, *see* aggression
Action for Children's Television, 70
aggression, 6, 8-9, 37, 38,
  41, 58-59, 79, 81
  action/adventure tele-
    vision shows and, 42,
    46, 47, 49-51, 59,
    60, 67
  educational television
    shows and, 43, 60
  high activity level and,
    61
  imagination and, 46, 55,
    60
  I.Q., and 47, 49, 56, 59
  orderliness of family life
    and, 53, 54, 55, 56,
    57, 59, 60
  personal achievement and,
    59, 85
  sex-role orientation and,
    61
  socioeconomic class and,
    46, 49, 53, 57, 61, 68

  television news shows and,
    46, 47
  television viewing and,
    38-39, 42-43, 46, 47,
    49-51, 53-55, 56-63,
    72, 124.
    in boys, 43, 51; in
    girls, 43, 51. *See also*
    television; television
    programming; television
    viewing
  See also family violence;
    violence
alcohol
  and interpersonal disputes,
    107-108, 110
  among Tahitians, 88
  among Tarahumara Indians,
    101-102
  violence and, 96-97, 108
American Medical Association,
  70
American Psychiatric Association, 70
animal studies, appli-
  cability to human violent
  behavior, 94
annual violence index, 70
armed forces, and violence,
  94, 98
arrest
  role of, 112-113
  tragic outcomes of, 117
  See also police
assault, 106, 108, 110, 113